Change Your Life Challenge

A 70 Day Life Makeover Program for Women

Change Your Life Challenge

A 70 Day Life Makeover Program for Women

Brook Noël

CHAMPION PRESS LTD.

CHAMPION PRESS, LTD.
FREDONIA, WISCONSIN

ISBN: 1932783091
LCCN: 2004110041

Manufactured in the United States of America

10 9 8 7 6 5 4 3 2 1

Acknowledgements

Every book is a combination of the people and experiences that have touched the author. This book contains the wisdom I have gleaned from many years and experiences.

I would like to acknowledge Scott Packowski and Anne Broomell who instilled in me the knowledge that we never "fail," but we do "fail upward." I learned that every experience in life teaches us something — if we are willing to learn.

To my wonderful husband, Andy, who has stood by me through a hundred reinventions, a thousand experiments, and my quest to always learn more, absorb more, live more, and laugh more. Thank you for always supporting my adventurous spirit.

To my brilliant and beautiful daughter Samantha, who has taught me more about the meaning of life than any book or sage ever could. You amaze me daily.

To my number one "fan," MaryAnn who reminds me daily that the stars are within my grasp.

To my wonderful big brother Caleb — you have inspired me to look at life with a fresh perspective. You have given me the gift of understanding the true value of a "moment."

To Chuck, who will probably hate being included in these acknowledgements, but such is life. You are an inspiration of strength and steadfastness, whether you want to be or not. So there.

To Sara, few are fortunate to know someone so caring, compassionate, supportive, and devoted. I am thankful for the decade that I have been able to call you my friend.

And last, but certainly not least, to my mother, whose support, wisdom, courage, and encouragement have always been the recipe from which I gather strength.

Dedication

I dedicate this journey to the 3000+ women who joined me online in testing the program. Your commitment to change is an inspiration to all. You are living proof that it only takes one person to change the world.

OTHER BOOKS BY BROOK NOEL:
Published by Champion Press, Ltd.(www.championpress.com)

Change Your Life Challenge Companion Workbook (ebook only)

Back to Basics:
101 Ideas for Strengthening Our Children and Our Families

The Ultimate Collection of Rush Hour Recipes:
Effortless Entertaining, Presto Pasta, Family Favorites and One-Pot Wonders (a "4 books in 1" cookbook)

Rush Hour Recipes:
Tips, Wisdom, and Recipes for Every Day of the Year

The Single Parent Manual

Grief Steps:
10 Steps to Regroup, Rebuild, and Renew After any Life Loss
Grief Steps Companion Workbook also available

I Wasn't Ready to Say Goodbye: Surviving, Coping, and Healing after the Sudden Death of a Loved One
(co-authored with Pamela D. Blair, PhD)
I Wasn't Ready to Say Goodbye Companion Workbook also available

Shadows of a Vagabond

Surviving Birthdays, Holidays and Anniversaries: A Guide to Grieving During Special Occasions

Living with Grief: A Guide to Your First Year of Grieving (co-authored with Pamela D. Blair, PhD)

Finding Peace: Exercises to Help Heal the Pain of Loss

You're Not Alone: Resource for the Grief Journey (co-authored with Pamela D. Blair, PhD)

Visit the author's websites at:
www.changeyourlifechallenge.com
www.rushhourcook.com
www.griefsteps.com

Be the change
you
want to see
in the world ...

-GOTHE

Contents

PART SIX: SUPER-MOM ... 211

This section looks at some common Mom-Dilemmas and offers simple strategies to restore sanity.

INTERMISSION: WOOD CHIPS, AN ESSAY ... 227

PART SEVEN: LIVING A SIMPLER LIFE ... 233

While the pace of our lives may never be "simple," we can simplify parts of our day and areas of our home. This three-day section provides basic skills for doing do so.

INTERMISSION: LAUGHTER ... 247

PART EIGHT: FOUNDATIONS OF FINANCIAL FREEDOM ... 249

Next to time, money is the single biggest stressor for people today. During these five days, we will take a hard look at your finances and place some controls on your spending and saving.

Why Does the 70-Day Challenge Work?

"Many people fail in life, not for lack of ability or brains or even courage but simply because they have never organized their energies around a goal."
Elbert Hubbard

If you are holding this book in your hands, you are ready to change either one aspect or many aspects of your life. Perhaps you are dissatisfied with your health or weight. Maybe you are exhausted and depressed and feeling overwhelmed by life's continuous treadmill. Perhaps your relationships are stale or draining or toxic — or maybe you don't have enough relationships in your life. Maybe you have been on the never-ending hunt for "something more." Whatever the area, you feel incomplete, but fortunately for us both, you aren't willing to give up. You have likely tried multiple programs, organizational systems, and self-help tools. Instead of realizing success, you likely realized money spent on a program that did not work longer than a month or two.

You have likely heard the saying, "takes one to know one ..." I was the aforementioned woman too. I was exhausted, stressed, worried, and dissatisfied with what my life had become in many ways. I purchased every system I could find to try and realize self-change. After a decade of building a self-help library that could lobby that of the Library of Congress, I paused and reflected on each of the books I had read, tapes to which I had listened, and theories I had tried. As I did these evaluations, I took a notebook and asked one question of each product: Why didn't this work for me? I quickly uncovered a pattern.

1. I tried to make a very big change at a time when my resources were depleted.

Often when we attempt to change, it is at a time when are not feeling that great about our self or our life to begin with. Who starts a diet when they are pleased with their body? We are more likely to start a diet after we try to squeeze into pants that once fit and discover that we can't even pull them past our knees. In this disenchanted state we try to revamp our food and exercise overnight. Then we become frustrated, damaging our self-esteem when we can't continue with these changes for more than several weeks (if that).

2. Programs rarely focus on multi-dimensional change.

Many programs focus on changing just your actions or just your thoughts. We don't become dissatisfied through just actions or just thoughts, but through a combination of wrong actions and destructive thoughts. In order to create any lasting change, we cannot alter just our thinking and assume that will take care of our actions. Likewise, we can't change our actions with the hope that our thoughts will also magically transform. We have to make a dual effort and take steps to change both thoughts and actions to create lasting lifestyle enhancement.

3. Many programs are too complicated!

Just because our lives are complicated, our programs do not need to be! Let's face it — much of our dissatisfaction is derived from lack of time. We don't have time to eat right, exercise, communicate with all of our friends, family, children, take walks, *etc.* A complicated system only compounds our internal confusion and frustration.

4. The action steps require a week's vacation.

I have attended many workshops and read through many books that had wonderful ideas — the only problem was that each action step would require a week off from work and family for proper implementation. Even when I could accomplish one step, undoubtedly life's pressures would bear down during the second week and I would have to abandoned the program. We are all working with 24/7 schedules and any practical, attainable program must recognize and fit within the many commitments we already have.

When I completed my analysis, I realized I had certainly tried enough systems and gathered a wealth of information. I decided to take these observations and create my own program, tailored to overcome the four stopping points I had uncovered. I wrote down each area I wanted to change and then began to take simple steps toward that change. I worked back and forth between changing thought and changing action. I learned to 'adapt versus desert' my program. Initially, I had no idea how long the program would take, but I was amazed to discover that in 70 days I was able to give my life a dramatic makeover.

Prior to writing this book, I spent eighteen months testing this program online. Over 2000 people took the Change Your Life Challenge. I used their comments and feedback to tweak and adjust the program even further. The most joyous moment of the process was discovering how this program helped the many women who were convinced that they had "tried everything" and "nothing else could possibly work." I believe you can finally accomplish the changes you desire and I believe that you can enjoy the journey, too!

How to Make the Change Your Life Challenge Work for You!

The Change Your Life Challenge was created as a step-by-step system. For that reason, it is important to follow the instructions as they are written. There are many books that can be opened randomly and a reader can begin anywhere. This is not one of them. In fact, if you try that approach, the system likely won't make any sense.

I also request that you follow the directions specifically. Some of the directions may seem "different" or unnatural — follow them anyway. You hold this book in your hands because the system you have is not working, or not working as well as you would like. Therefore, I ask you to try these ideas as invented. Many people who have completed this challenge successfully, initially thought that certain instructions would never work for their lifestyle. Once they worked through the challenge, they realized otherwise. Once you complete the entire challenge, then you are free to modify, customize, and adjust the "rules" to fit your needs. We cover this more in-depth at the end of the challenge.

Do not be pressured by the description "70-Day." There is not a hard and fast rule that this program must be completed in 70 days. If you find that schedule to be too intimidating or aggressive, then work on doing one step every other day or every three days. It is important to finish the program by working through the assignments at a regular interval. While you can complete the challenge in longer than 70 days, I highly caution against trying to-do the challenge more quickly. True lifestyle changes are built through time and consistency. Trying to accelerate that process is the primary reason people fail.

When Do I Start the Program?

When I did the program for the first time, I began on a Monday. I would do five days of challenges and then use the weekend to "catch up" or relax. I suggest the same format for your challenge. I have also added "Intermissions" to the challenge. These are additional thought-provoking ideas or reading that I thought would be valuable to you. You can read these Intermissions whenever you choose.

Find a Partner

A partner can be a crucial step for any successful program of change. When we are run-down or ready to give in, a partner can act as a cheerleader to spur us forward. Likewise, everything is easier when we realize someone is in a similar place, at a similar time, facing similar challenges. There are many areas of this challenge where working with another person will also make the challenge more fun. Go ahead and ask around. I think you will be surprised at how many people are looking to take more control of their time and their life.

Certificate of Sanity

For all who successfully finish the challenge, a Certificate of Sanity is waiting for you. While a paper reward will be less gratifying than the personal change you will realize in your life, it is a little gift from me to you to recognize your commitment and your achievement. You'll find more information about this Certificate of Sanity at the end of the book. Just follow the directions and your certificate will be on its way in the mail.

Other Notes

I have created a *Change Your Life Challenge Companion Workbook*, which contains blank worksheets and additional companion pages needed for this challenge. With the size of the book in your hands, I thought a letter-size format for worksheets would be useful for many. This is only available as an ebook. I chose this format so users could print additional copies of worksheets as needed. This workbook can be downloaded immediately at www.changeyourlifechallenge.com. Throughout this book you will see a ✏ symbol to denote a corresponding page in the *Change Your Life Challenge Workbook.* It is not necessary to purchase the workbook in order to complete the challenge, although it makes the preparation and printing of worksheets easier. The workbook also contains a few bonus challenges, pre-designed meal plans, and other tools you can combine with your challenge.

Abbreviations

To reduce redundancy, you will find the following abbreviations in this book:

CYLC Binder: This refers to the master binder you will create on Day 3.

CYLC: This abbreviation stands for Change Your Life Challenge.

Setting Up Shop

"Don't let the fear of the time it will take to accomplish something stand in the way of your doing it. The time will pass anyway; we might just as well put that passing time to the best possible use."
Earl Nightingale, speaker, author

All long-term successes are built on solid foundations. Most of the time, when we implement a change, we want the change to occur *now*. In our eagerness to realize change, we often skip the process of building a solid foundation. We begin with a "go-get 'em" attitude, only to crumble a few days or weeks later when our foundation is faulty.

Since you didn't get into an organizational upheaval overnight, keep in mind that it takes baby steps to get out. The premise of this program is that simple efforts, made daily, will yield big results over time

You may be asking yourself, "What am I getting myself into?" "Is it worth it?" You bet. In 70 days you'll feel like you have had a complete life makeover — as long as you make a consistent, focused effort on the daily challenges.

For starters, we need to make sure you have your basic supplies together. Throughout the challenge, you will likely want to purchase a few additional inexpensive items, but the following supply list includes all the basic must-have items.

Change Your Life Challenge Supply List

- (2) three-ring binders, one-inch capacity
- (1) three-ring binder, half-inch capacity
- Several folders or pockets to insert on the rings of your three-ring binders
- A monthly or weekly calendar on 8.5 x 11 hole-punched paper
- Loose-leaf, lined paper
- A brightly colored, letter-size, wire-spiral notebook, single subject (with the holes — so pages can be easily transferred into your binder)
- Index cards (lined or unlined, any color)
- A phone message book (preferably one with two forms and carbon)
- Dry erase markers (one color for each family member)
- A dry erase board that is half corkboard (I found these inexpensively at Wal-Mart)
- Push pins (for the corkboard)
- Stapler
- Tape
- Glue stick
- Scissors
- Red pen
- Yellow highlighter
- Hanging files
- Manila files
- One crate that holds hanging files
- Plastic sheet protectors

- (2) sets of eight blank tabs for your binders
- A wire basket or container to use as an in-box
- Four large RubberMaid® (or other brand of your choice) plastic tubs. (You can save money by using cardboard boxes, although I find a durable tub to be a better choice.)

There are a few more things that we will get later in the journey — but those are best purchased later as you customize your system.

Change Your Life Support

Partners: If you have a friend, colleague, or co-worker that would work through the challenge with you, purchase or ask them to purchase a copy of this book and start at the same time. One of the best ways I've found to stick with anything is to have an accountability partner.

Web Site: The Change Your Life Challenge website (www.changeyourlifechallenge.com) offers tips, wisdom, a free newsletter, and other information and support.

Understanding the Program

The challenge is divided into 11 phases. Each phase covers a different life area. The basic premise is to first deal with the current upheaval in your life — both internal and external — before moving into other life areas. Here is a summary of the challenge phases.

Part One (twelve days)

The Change Your Life Challenge Toolbox: A Twelve-Day Sprint to Becoming More Organized and Using Time Wisely

From procrastination to an effective "communication station" this section covers the vital steps for a solid program foundation. You will also learn a few simple techniques to improve your outlook on life.

Part Two (eight days)

The Nitty-Gritty: Dealing With the In-House Backlog

Before we can design a system to carry us forward, we have to deal with the backlog in our households. This section offers tried-and-true methods for household maintenance, managing tasks, and beautifying your home.

Part Three (five days)

Information Management

Every home has to handle paper and information effectively in order to run at its maximum efficiency. You'll learn about several systems for information management and how to adapt the one most suited for your family needs.

Part Four (five days)

Recreating the Family Dinner

Whether you belong to a family of one, two, or twenty, managing the dinner hour proves a difficult task for many. This section will walk you through the steps to creating master meal plans, shopping lists, and everything else needed for a sane and simple dinner hour.

Part Five (ten days)

Relationships, Romance, and Friendships

Who we spend our time with, and how we spend that time is the single largest external factor affecting our quality of life. This section examines how we spend our time, with whom we spend it , and how that affects us. Additionally, we begin implementing positive change where needed.

Part Six (four days)

Super-Mom

This section looks at some common Mom-Dilemmas and offers simple strategies to restore sanity.

Part Seven (four days)

Living a Simpler Life

While the pace of our lives may never be "simple," we can simplify parts of our day and areas of our home. This three-day section provides basic skills for doing so.

Part Eight (five days)

Money Management

Next to time, money is the single biggest stressor for people today. During these five days, we will take a hard look at your finances and place some controls on your spending and saving.

Part Nine (six days)
To Your Health
If we are not healthy and functioning at our healthiest level, then we cannot optimally care for others. During these six days, we will implement simple steps to maximize health and energy.

Part Ten (seven days)
How to Take Care of Your Self,
While Taking Care of Every One Else
As we near the end of the challenge, we take an in-depth look at how you care for your self. Nurturing your mind, body, and soul will play a vital role in the continuation of your success after you close this book.

Part Eleven (three days)
Something More
We cannot build a complete life within a bubble. Contentment and fulfillment come from connecting our balanced world with the world of others. These three days explore the importance of connecting with a mission extending beyond the four walls within which we live.

Daily Routine Action Lists

Throughout the challenge, we will be adding new "routine" activities. To make this challenge as easy as possible, you will find a summary of the "new habits" we will develop inside the first page of each section of the challenge. This list will summarize what activities are to be added and when, and will serve as a hand reference for staying on course. These lists do not include tasks that are only done once. The list only includes tasks or assignments that will become a part of your daily routine.

Setting Up Shop: A Five-Step Summary

1. Make sure you have all of your basic supplies.
2. Review the program you are about to embark on.
3. Find a partner (if you haven't already).
4. Visit the Change Your Life Challenge website to familiarize yourself with additional tools.
5. Purchase the downloadable workbook if you would like additional worksheets and support at www.changeyourlifechallenge.com

Part One
The Change Your Life Challenge Toolbox

A Twelve-Day Sprint to Becoming More Organized and Using Time Wisely

Daily Routine Action List

Days Two and Three:

- ☐ Begin each day with a heartfelt "good morning."

Day Four:

- ☐ Begin each day with a heartfelt "good morning."
- ☐ Begin carrying your CATCH-ALL notebook with you everywhere.

Day Five:

- ☐ Begin each day with a heartfelt "good morning."
- ☐ Carry your CATCH-ALL notebook with you everywhere.
- ☐ Begin transferring your to-do list each night.

Day Six:

- ☐ Begin each day with a heartfelt "good morning."
- ☐ Carry your CATCH-ALL notebook with you everywhere.
- ☐ Transfer your to-do list each night.
- ☐ Begin doing a Nightly Reflection each evening.

Days Seven through Twelve:

- ☐ Begin each day with a heartfelt "good morning."
- ☐ Carry your CATCH-ALL notebook with you everywhere.
- ☐ Transfer your to-do list each night.
- ☐ Complete your Nightly Reflection each evening.
- ☐ Each day, use the three-step action list.

Day 1
The "Before" Snapshot

✵

"I am looking forward to looking back on all of this."
Unknown

I hate to start off with a cliché, but I will nonetheless: "Before we can change where we are going, we must understand where we are, and where we have been." We don't want to make the same mistake we have in the past, that of jumping into "yet another solution" because we are unhappy with some aspect of our life. When we spontaneously jump into change, we set ourselves up for failure in two ways; (1) We don't stop and truly assess what we *want* to change; (2) We don't look at our life in its entirety to see what *needs* to be changed.

Oftentimes we will buy a book, workbook, or audiotape because the topic or "promise" strikes a chord. On a whim, we make the purchase hoping that it will help us create change. Usually, it doesn't. However, this is likely more a reflection of our own approach to change, than the content of the book or audiotape. When we approach any change without clearly identifying our needs, our needs will be almost impossible fulfill. We can't find an answer to an undefined question.

Today we will be taking a "snapshot" of your life. Don't cringe and close the cover, I realize this isn't going to be a glorious snapshot — if it was, you wouldn't be taking the challenge. That's okay.

I was hardly satisfied when I began the concept of this program. In fact, if it weren't for my dissatisfaction this program wouldn't have been created.

Think of this "snapshot" as your "before" picture. It isn't supposed to be "pretty." Rest assured that in 70 days you will have quite the "after." This snapshot will be an invaluable tool for measuring your progress throughout the program. It is also a great reference for reminding yourself why you began this endeavor when you are knee-deep in hand-me-downs, evaluating your mission, sorting through mismatched Tupperware® lids, and trying to get out of bed a bit earlier to take a walk.

To create your snapshot you will need to complete the worksheet in the Appendix. This worksheet is also included in the *Change Your Life Challenge Workbook.*

How to Complete the Worksheet

While this may sound complicated, rest assured my nine-year-old tested these instructions and made if through just fine. Make sure to have a copy of the worksheet nearby while reading through the instructions.

The worksheet is broken down into different life areas. These are the areas that we will be working through in our 70-Day Challenge. Above each area there is a column of boxes numbered one through ten. These columns are "priority scales." A one means that this area is not that important to you at this period in your life. A ten means this area is very important to you.

Begin by carefully considering each column. Decide how important that specific "life area" is to you. Where would you like to ultimately be on the scale? For example, when I completed my snapshot, "time with family" was something that I really needed to develop. Once you have made your decision, take your red marker and make a line where you would like to be. I chose to make a red line between the nine and ten in that column.

A word of warning before you go marking up your worksheet: Make sure you are choosing what will make YOU content — not what others want for you, or what will make others happy. As women, we often fall into the "please everyone — sacrifice ourselves" trap. We want to be everything to everyone and then we ride the rollercoaster of guilt when we can't live up to this high standard. I know what that snapshot looks like — I've tried it. I don't want to see that on your worksheet. Instead, I want you to try something that might be a bit foreign. For each area consider what *you* truly want from *your* life, and place your red line at that measure. Odds are you won't want or need to achieve a ten in every area of your life (even though many of us try). Instead of hunting down elusive perfection, give careful consideration to what is important to you. Many times we think we should be able to accomplish many things — but we never question *why*. Perhaps we were raised in a spotless home where dinner was always on the table by five and we strive to continue those practices in our own home. But ask yourself: *Is having an absolutely spotless home a necessity to my contentment?* If not, lower the bar (the red line). Maybe it isn't that important to you, but it is important to those you live with. We will deal with those conflicts later — right now just focus on what is important to *you*.

Remember that we also go through seasons in our lives. Respect these seasons. There have been times in my life when work was a ten and children were a ten, but my relationship was a five. My husband and I were both very busy within our demanding jobs and we didn't have as much time as either of us wished to spend together. A year later, that changed and my relationship became a ten on my list and work moved down a notch. While I realize some people may recoil in horror that I committed to ink the fact that at a point in my life work was a higher priority than my husband, guess what? That is life. If I am working ninety hours per week, I can hardly be the perfect wife. To expect or attempt to be will only lead to feelings of guilt. That is not to say I do not love my husband completely — I certainly do. It does show however, a realization and acceptance of the simple fact: *Life comes in seasons and there will be times when I have to focus on one important area over another.*

I love the quote, "You can have it all — just not all at the same time." Sure, in fairy tales and dreamland, everything is a perfect ten and we can balance and maintain everything perfectly. Until we figure out how to get a ticket to that world and leave reality behind, we must shatter these illusions and join the real world.

Keep in mind that no one has to see this snapshot. It is just for you. Carefully consider this starting tool and take your time — it will be very important to your overall program progress.

After you have carefully considered each column and marked each with a red line, grab your yellow highlighter. Use this pen to color in blocks to represent where you are currently. For example, if redoing your diet is a high priority in your life, you may have given it a nine or ten for importance with your red marker. In looking at your current behaviors, you might be eating truffles and Twinkies® twenty times a day. Obviously, in that case you would only color in one or two squares. Continue working through each area, giving careful consideration to where you are currently.

Go ahead and hole punch your worksheet and place it behind the SNAPSHOT tab in the Change Your Life Challenge Binder you purchased as part of the "Setting Up Shop" assignment. (We will get to the rest of the supplies soon enough.)

As you look at your snapshot, think through, or better yet, write out your answers to the following questions:

✎ These questions and space for the answers can be found in the *Companion Workbook*.

1. What areas have the biggest imbalance between where you are and where you would like to be ultimately? Why do you think that is?
2. What systems have you tried in the past?
3. Our stress is normally caused by imbalances in our life. Looking at the chart, what stressor do you realize has been playing a big part in your life? Are you ready and willing to change it?
4. Are you trying to be Superwoman? How many tens did you mark with red pen? If you have more than three, perhaps you are trying to have it all *now*. Think through your life again and carefully consider the current "season" of your life. Realize that you can change this sheet in a week, a month, a quarter.

Where are your biggest imbalances? As a result which items should be your "10s" for this phase of your life?

If You Are Having a Hard Time Defining Your Tens

Sometimes all the "noise" in our heads makes it difficult to truly decipher our own needs and intentions. We can't differentiate what we want versus what others want for us, or what we "think" we should want. If you are suffering from this syndrome, take out a piece of paper and recall times where you felt excess stress, worry, or guilt in the last thirty days. After creating this list, write down next to each item what "category" it would fall into from the choices on the SNAPSHOT worksheet. Our strongest emotions arise from the areas we feel most strongly about. Whichever category contained the most items from this list is likely to be the ten for this season of your life.

Your snapshot is now complete — and so is Day One. That wasn't so hard was it?

WARNING

Usually when we start a program like the CYLC it is at a time when we are fed-up or frustrated with some aspect of our lives. We want change — and we want it NOW! (You know if you are one of these people because you already have your thumb and finger ready to turn to Day Two — even though it is still Day One.) I want to caution you against moving forward before a new day dawns. It is this overzealousness that so often leads to burnout when we are only one-third or halfway to our goal. When we tested the challenge online, it was easy to see who was "skipping ahead," and I don't recall one of those "skippers" completing the program. This program is designed to be handled one-day-at-a-time. I did not test it with people who worked through twenty days in the first 10 minutes, then skipped a week, then did another ten days. I tested this as a carefully plotted, consistent effort over a 70-day period (plus weekends). If you want to realize the positive change that this program can offer in your life, follow the program as it is intended and then pick up one of these suggested reads. (Or you can explore one of the Intermissions between challenge phases. These Intermissions can be completed whenever the mood strikes you.) When you want to push forward in positive change, put this book down after your daily assignment and pick up one of these enlightening books instead.

Suggested Reading:

The Tao of Womanhood: Ten Lessons for Power and Peace by Diane Dreher (ISBN: 0688166296)

Voice of Her Own: Women and the Journal Writing Journey by Marlene A. Schiwy (ISBN: 0684803429)

Common-Sense Organizing: A Step-by-Step Guide for Taking Control of Your Life by Debbie Williams (ISBN: 1932783261)

What Happy People Know: How the New Science of Happiness Can Change Your Life for the Better by Dan Baker (ISBN: 0312321597)

Take Time for Your Life by Cheryl Richardson (ISBN: 0767902076)

The Four Agreements: A Practical Guide to Personal Freedom by Miguel Ruiz (ISBN: 1878424319)

Your Assignment

Complete the Before Snapshot exercise.

Day 2
How Do You Start Your Day?

✵

"Sunshine is delicious, rain is refreshing, wind braces up, snow is exhilarating; there is no such thing as bad weather, only different kinds of good weather."
John Ruskin

As I mentioned in the introduction (which you should read if you haven't already) lasting change is only realized when we work on both how we think and how we act. Many programs fail because they tackle only thought or only action. Often we try to compartmentalize and change just one area of our life. We might focus on communication or cholesterol or calories or cardio. However the areas of our life do not operate in a vacuum. Sure, we can maintain a compartmentalized change for a few weeks, months, or even years — but ultimately we must change the other components of our life to create lasting change.

For this reason, you will see that the CYCL works back and forth between practical action steps and practical steps to change how we think. Today we will take a simple step toward changing our thought patterns. This very simple assignment can work wonders in your life. Imagine this scene with me:

> Your alarm goes off and you struggle to get out of bed on time as the electronic beeping pierces your eardrum.

Your first thought is "When is daylight savings?" How you would love the extra hour. With the realization that it just occurred a month ago, you stumble to your feet and head toward the shower. After showering and dressing you go downstairs to find your family at the breakfast table. "Good morning," you say as enthusiastically as possible for 6:00 AM. You are greeted with a few moments of silence, then a half-hearted "hello" before everyone returns to his or her breakfast bowls and conversation. You grab a cup of coffee and a muffin to have on your way to work. While driving to work your cell phone rings. It is your best friend from college. After a cursory hello she breaks into an auctioneer ramble. "I'm really in a jam. My babysitter called and she is sick. Can you watch my kids tonight for thirty minutes while I run and pick up Jacob's present?"

Always there for one another, you tell her you would be happy to watch Jacob before hanging up the phone. You get to work and find someone in your designated parking place. Frustrated, your "okay mood" is drastically deteriorating. You park near the back of the lot only to step into a wad of gum as you get out of the car. *UGH,* you think, *it's going to be one of those days.*

You shuffle into the office, passing the receptionist. Normally she welcomes you with a cheerful greeting, but today she is busy taking notes while talking on the phone and doesn't offer so much as a nod. You sigh again and trod to the meeting room.

Have you imagined this scene? Any idea what is missing? Two simple words: GOOD MORNING (backed by sincerity and enthusiasm).

The first thirty to sixty minutes of our day set the tone for the hours to come. Getting off to a cheerful start has a dramatic impact on how our day will flow.

Your Assignment

Let today be the last day that you have not said "good morning" to *yourself* and the last day that you begin your life on "auto-pilot." Tomorrow when you awake, don't jump into a crazy-pace and forget the crucial step of giving yourself a "morning hello." Before you even get out of bed, take a few deep breaths and say "Good morning." Run through your positive qualities. Say a quick prayer. Focus on your day ahead and imagine moving through it effortlessly. Research has shown that those who visualize their day beforehand have a much better success ratio than those who do not. Look in the mirror and smile. While showering, think of five things you are grateful for. While getting dressed, develop curiosity about the day. Try saying, "I know something wonderful will happen today ... I can't wait to see what it is."

Try to spend at least three minutes each morning doing positive-thought activities. It might be awkward at first, but stick with it. Likewise, remember that you have a great impact on everyone around you — especially in the morning. Breakfast is considered a vital physical component of getting our day off to a good start. Likewise, a positive morning routine is vital to getting our day off to a positive emotional start.

There is an interesting phenomenon that you will likely notice when recollecting your life or examining the lives of others with whom you are close. If we think the day is going to be "not so good," we will likely be right. If we think the day will "be great," we will likely be right. Our thoughts about what is to come act like a magnet — thus the cliché "What we think about, we bring about."

Take a moment to reflect on your morning thought patterns. Can you detect a correlation between your thoughts and what is happening in your life right now?

This program is about change — changing our external environment, aligning our life with our priorities, and creating internal change to support the external. Feeling good about ourselves is a necessity for implementing any lasting change. When something makes us feel good we are much more likely to stick with it — that is why it's so important to focus not just on your external surroundings — but on your internal approach as well.

Day 3

The Change Your Life Challenge Headquarters

✵

"A man who dares to waste one hour of life has not discovered the value of life."
Charles Darwin

Hopefully you have purchased the supplies in the "Setting Up Shop" section. If not, take a quick trip to your local Wal-Mart or office supply store as we are going to set up your Change Your Life Challenge Headquarters today. Throughout the challenge, you will be modifying and adding to this "base."

First, you must choose a location. I recommend an area that is centrally located, without being in a high-traffic zone. The last thing we want to happen is for your "beautiful base" to be rummaged through by a family member hunting down tape or a scissors. If you are short on space, consider storing all of your supplies in a crate. You can transfer this crate into a closet or beneath a desk for safekeeping and take it out as needed.

Next, take out your white tabs and one of the two (one-inch capacity) binders you purchased. Label the tabs with the following categories:

SNAPSHOT

CONTACTS

REFERENCE

SHOPPING LISTS

RECIPES

MASTER TASK LIST

CALENDAR

BUDGET

Insert these tabs onto the rings. Place some white lined paper in the back of the binder.

Place your purchased calendar pages behind the calendar tab. Download a CONTACT page (or create your own) and place ten to twenty copies behind the CONACT tab.

Place all of the supplies you have purchased into a drawer or crate for easy access.

✎ Contact pages are available in the *Companion Workbook*.

Your Assignment

Complete the set up of your Change Your Life Challenge Head-quarters.

Day 4
The Catch-All Notebook

"Look at your past. Your past has determined where you are at this moment. What you do today will determine where you are tomorrow."
Tom Hopkins

Today you are going to meet your new best friend ... the CATCH-ALL notebook. Before you meet this dandy new friend, let me tell you about my typical day. I am the CEO of a company, mother of one, wife to one (thank goodness), founder of a bereavement 24/7 support site, church volunteer, in-training for a marathon, and the author of over a dozen books. Did I mention I also have two golden retriever puppies (sisters), two cats, and a bunny? (My daughter keeps talking about a horse — but so far I've won that battle.)

I average over 2000 emails per day and fifty phone calls. At any given time, I oversee our company's book line with over forty new books in various stages of production. I am blessed with a wonderful, although small staff, which can handle just about anything with their eyes closed. My husband travels two to four days per week, but when he is home he is also a great "helper-outer."

Why am I sharing all this? It isn't a brag-fest, I wouldn't wish my responsibility on anyone nor would I change the hectic pace of my life (this is the season I am in right now). I am sharing this because over the years, hundreds of people have said, "I don't know how you do it! What's the secret?" I am convinced the CATCH-ALL notebook is key to juggling all of these tasks. Amazingly, I rarely forget anything and I keep everything moving forward smoothly. This notebook will help you create an effective environment, to never forget anything, and will your functioning at maximum potential.

I think our biggest mistake in organizing is attempting to make our systems too complicated. Just because our lives are complicated does not mean our systems have to be. I have tried keeping files for each day of the week, index systems, electronic information devices, and many other handy-dandy-organizing gadgets, only to lose the Tuesday folder, accidentally send a note to school on the back of my Wednesday to-do card, or forget to change my batteries and lose all the information stored in my $500 fool-proof-gadget. The CYLC Binder and the CATCH-ALL notebook are my key supplies. The binder acts as a "base" that never moves and the CATCH-ALL acts like "special forces" sent out to accompany me on my daily missions.

So what do I put in this notebook? EVERYTHING! (That's why I nicknamed it the CATCH-ALL Notebook.)

How to Use Your CATCH-ALL Notebook

My guess is that this will be a foreign way of tracking your to-do items compared to what you have done or tried in the past. Since your past efforts have left you at a place where you are seeking out the Change Your Life Challenge it is important to be open to a new system — even if it seems a bit out-of-the-ordinary. (This is likely to be the most complicated day of the challenge. Once you have this system down, you will be ready to go!)

Leave the first page of the binder blank. Starting on the second page, create the following categories by writing each phrase at the top of the page. Write one phrase on each page (consecutively so there are no blank pages between them). If you have done this correctly, you will have seven pages after the blank page.

1. LONG-TERM PROJECTS
2. SHORT-TERM PROJECTS
3. SHORT-TERM TO-DO's
4. LONG-TERM TO-DO's
5. SHORT TERM REFERENCE
6. LONG TERM REFERENCE
7. DELEGATED

Let's look at each page in more detail and at its purpose in your system.

PROJECTS VERSUS TO-DOs: For the sake of this challenge we identify TO-DOs as any simple tasks that can be completed in one or two steps. You will record these in list form on either the SHORT-TERM or LONG-TERM TO-DO list. The SHORT-TERM TO-DO list is for tasks that can (or will) be completed in the next sixty days. The LONG-TERM TO-DO list is for tasks that can (or will) take 61 days or more.

The reason we group to-do items separately from projects (which often take weeks or months to complete) is that if we don't, we end up with a long list where we are rarely able to cross off an item. When we don't see action, we are likely to abandoned ship. The SHORT TERM TO-DO list becomes an actionable list that you can cross off easily.

To summarize: if your task can be completed in one or two steps it goes on a TO-DO list. If it is something you need to-do within the next sixty days, put it on the SHORT-TERM list. If it's something more than sixty days out, put it on the LONG-TERM TO-DO list.

PROJECTS: A project is defined as any task requiring more than two steps for completion. For example, doing a load of laundry would fall under the SHORT-TERM TO-DO list whereas a complete spring-cleaning would be a PROJECT. For each project decide if it is short-term (to be done within the next sixty days) or long-term (more than sixty days out) and write it on the appropriate page. When you get to the point where you are actively pursuing the project (for example, you are ready to spring clean) you would break down the tasks and transfer them to your SHORT-TERM to-do list. Don't worry — you don't have to plan any cleaning yet. That will be covered later in the challenge. Today's goal is simply to understand the different categories of our CYLC Binder.

If you think of your life like a movie, it's easy to understand the purpose of these lists. On a film or television set, the most compelling pieces are made with multiple cameras. If a studio only has one camera, viewers can only see the people on the set from one angle. You have probably seen shows like this on your public access station where everything is filmed head on.

For major projects (and our life is a major project) studios use multiple cameras and alternate between the cameras to get the best view of the set. Our lists serve as cameras offering different views of our lives and everything within them. Each list should be easy to locate and scan through quickly, which is why I don't promote super in-depth referencing or multiple notebooks. There is a fine line between *too simple* where something isn't functional, and *so detailed* something isn't functional. Imagine if a set had 30 cameras on it! That wouldn't make a movie more interesting — it would just make it more confusing.

Some projects may warrant a full page in your notebook. If you are planning a family vacation, you will likely have a lot of confirmation numbers, flight dates, times, and other information to track. For information-intensive projects, leave a full page with the project name at the top, *i.e.*, "Family Vacation." This allows a quick and easy way to find the information you are seeking.

So what we end up with is a glance at our current commitments through the SHORT-TERM TO-DOs and SHORT-TERM PROJECTS and a glimpse into the future through our LONG-TERM TO-DOs and LONG-TERM PROJECT list.

SHORT-TERM REFERENCE: Your short-term reference page is where you list all the little things that you may need at your fingertips in the near future. Keep in mind that this list is in your CATCH-ALL notebook which is going with you throughout the day. Your CYLC Binder (your master planning station which we covered in

Day 3) never moves. It lives in your house and must be left there. While you go throughout your day, you capture anything that will be transferred into the master station on your short-term reference page. When you get a new phone number and address you would write it down here and then transfer it into your binder at night (we will cover this "NIGHTLY RELFECTION" the day after tomorrow). If you place an order by phone, you would write the order number here in case there is a problem and you need to call with a question about the order. If there is a book you hear about and would like to read you could write down the title on your SHORT-TERM REFERENCE (if you think you'll read it within the next sixty days) or in the LONG-TERM reference if it will be later than sixty days. Perhaps a friend tells you of a new web site where vitamins are fifty percent off — that would go in your reference list. If you sign up for a new service on the Internet, write down your user name and password on your SHORT-TERM reference page. (I'll show you what to-do with all this information in the nightly reflection.)

LONG-TERM REFERENCE: This page collects all those things that you don't want to forget, but don't need to remember this instant. This is like the "hard drive" of your computer. Placing things on this list helps to remove them from your current focus and free up memory. If you are scanning through a magazine and come across a convention you would like to attend in eight months, record the information here so not to lose it. Maybe you see something that would make a great gift but the gift-giving time isn't for another four months, record the information on this page. Maybe you are thinking about enrolling your child in summer camp, but it's the dead of winter when a friend mentions a great camp program — write it down here.

THE DELEGATED PAGE: How many times have you turned something over to someone else to handle only to discover they dropped the ball? Unfortunately, since you turned it over to someone else, you assumed he or she would take care of the task and you deleted it from your brain's hard drive. The DELEGATED page acts as a space to record these types of tasks. I used to just leave these items on my TO-DO or PROJECT list but would get frustrated when I had twenty things TO-DO and fifteen of them were in the hands of someone else. Now I keep these tasks separate. Here are a few examples from my current DELEGATED list:

1. Andy (husband): Call and figure out why Company XYX is charging us double every month.
2. Webmaster: Build an HTML page for the Women in Wellness site.
3. Create posters for Book Expo America (currently with the designer).

These are examples where I can't take any action steps, but I still need to monitor them at some level to make sure they get done. Make sure to write on your DELEGATED page "who" is in charge of each item and their phone or email (if applicable). You may also want to write down when you expect to hear back as an indication of when you should follow up.

On a side note, one of the most successful organizing strategies I have come across is "Keep Like Items Together." That is the main reason we separate these different tasks onto different pages. When we jumble them all together it becomes a hodge-podge list and difficult to find what you need, when you need it. Likewise, if you over-organize you face the same problem. Each of these pages requires a different type of thought process. The SHORT-TERM TO-DO page requires action-oriented thinking. The DELEGATED page requires follow-up and follow-through skills. The PROJECT page requires planning and systematic thinking. By keeping like items together, we are able to stay focused in one specific mindset and move through the items more quickly.

In summary, everything you need or want to-do, and everything you need or want to remember, should go in this notebook. (And yes, they do fill up quickly! You will archive these eventually.)

WARNING: *Do not try to get fancy and have a notebook for family matters, a notebook for work matters, etc. Just use one notebook.*

Now that you have met your CATCH-ALL Notebook, these are the things you should no longer do ...

- I will no longer say "I don't need to write that down, because I will remember it."
- I will no longer use sticky-notes or other small papers with adhesive to jot down notes, messages, and the like.

- I will no longer write on the nearest paper or envelope or wrinkled corner of whatever is handy.
- I will no longer take a piece of valuable information from somewhere (*i.e.* business card, phone number) unless I first record it in my CATCH-ALL notebook. (Or you can tape or staple the card to a page.)
- I will no longer go anywhere without my CATCH-ALL notebook.

Your Assignment

Today, begin carrying your CATCH-ALL notebook with you EVERYWHERE. Start recording information in your CATCH-ALL per the instructions. We are all constantly barraged with items that need to be handled; recording these items on paper greatly frees our focusing ability.

You may be wondering: *What goes on page one which I left blank?* I like to put a favorite quote on page one — something I find inspirational and motivating. Or make a list of things you like about yourself. Your first page should be devoted to something light and fun! On the front or back cover, write the date you started this notebook. (These notebooks will eventually be archived.) Whenever you complete the notebook, write the end date.

A Fun Place to Explore

As you build your calendars and contacts, try visiting www.pcworld.com and clicking on DOWNLOADS. Then search for CALENDAR, or ADDRESSES, or ORGANIZE. You will find many free pages that can be downloaded to help with your organizational needs. You will also find additional, reproducible pages that I have created in the *Change Your Life Challenge Workbook.* ✐

Day 5
The Trick to Never Forgetting Anything

✵

"If you do not change directions, you may end up where you are heading."
Lao-Tzu

Here is the key to never forgetting anything, which also helps end procrastination. Look at your SHORT-TERM TO-DO list in your CATCH-ALL notebook. Cross off any completed items. Take everything left on the SHORT-TERM list and move it to a fresh page. Even if the list is fifty items long, rewrite it. Re-writing serves three primary purposes:

1. It ensures that you won't overlook anything.
2. It keeps all the "active items" fresh on your mind.
3. There are certain tasks, that for whatever reason, we don't like doing. These items tend to stay on a to-do list for a long, long time. We get used to just glancing them over and looking at the next item that we *want* to-do. When you rewrite "FERTILIZE THE LAWN" for thirty consecutive days it will really begin to grate on your nerves. I guarantee that one day a little piece of you will wake up DETERMINED to cross off that item. Each time you rewrite a TO-DO item; you are planting a little

action seed in your subconscious. One day that seed will bloom and voila — you can cross the item from your list.

I know it sounds repetitive — but trust me, this is a big key in keeping all your tasks organized and completing them.

Your Assignment

Each night, transfer your to-do items in your CATCH-ALL notebook.

Day 6
The Nightly Reflection

✵

"The real voyage of discovery consists not in seeking new landscapes, but having new eyes."
Marcel Proust

Starting this evening, you'll be doing a NIGHTLY REFLECTION that will take about ten minutes.

The first goal of the NIGHTLY REFLECTION is to take the daily information from the CATCH-ALL notebook and transfer it to the CYLC Headquarters. Information to be transferred would include:

APPOINTMENTS into your calendar
CONTACTS into your contact pages
REFERENCE materials
NEWLY DELEGATED tasks or activities

Next check the following:

1. Are there any LONG-TERM projects you need to move to the SHORT-TERM page?
2. Any SHORT-TERM projects you have delayed that need to be moved to the LONG-TERM list?
3. Were any of the DELEGATED items completed?

If DELEGATED items weren't completed, do you need to call anyone to follow up? If so, add it to your SHORT-TERM TO-DO LIST. (It will still stay on your DELEGATED list until it is completely finished. Likewise when you break down projects into steps, you put the steps on your TO-DO list but don't cross the project off until it is TOTALLY completed. This way, when considering a new challenge, task, or responsibility, you can quickly glance at your PROJECT lists to assess what is already on your plate.)

TIP: *Because you will be rewriting your SHORT-TERM TO-DO LIST regularly (there is no need to re-write any of the other lists) you will end up with most of your lists grouped together — then a bunch of scratched out pages — and then your SHORT-TERM TO-DO list. For easy reference, place a paper clip where your main lists are and then another on your SHORT TERM TO-DO list.*

Last Step

Before you go to bed each night, make sure you have emptied out that racing mind. What are you thinking about? Is it something you need to-do? If yes, is it on one of your lists? Much of our stress stems from trying to juggle so many tasks. Consider your CATCH-ALL notebook your "back up brain." Once you have recorded something in your notebook, give yourself permission to quit thinking about it. This takes a bit of practice, but as you see the system working for you, it will become easier.

Your Assignment

Complete your first nightly reflection using the guidelines provided today. Choose when you will be doing your NIGHTLY RELFECTION each night from this point forward. I like to-do mine moments before I go to bed. That gives me a way to get everything that is whirring around in my brain on paper so I can have a peaceful night's sleep.

Day 7
Priority Planning and the Three-Step Action List

"Don't mistake movement for achievement.
It's easy to get faked out by being busy.
The question is: Busy doing what?"
Jim Rohn

Today you will learn about one of the easiest systems ever invented for simple priority planning and staying on track in creating the life you desire. If you have not completed the SNAPSHOT from Day One, you must stop and complete that worksheet before proceeding.

As you work in your CATCH-ALL notebook, you will likely create TO-DO lists that hold many items. Many of the items on the list will be somewhat important, but only a few will be VERY important. You are probably familiar with the priority planning systems where items are coded A, B, or C based on their importance. That's too much work for me as my lists are too long. I've developed a simple system that allows me to stay focused in the daily rush of life and take even larger strides toward what I want to achieve.

What I'd like you to-do is scan your entire SHORT-TERM TO-DO list. Now, choose three things that you will do TOMORROW. (This will be part of your NIGHTLY REFLECTION routine from now on.) When choosing, ask yourself: *If I were to get NOTHING but three things done tomorrow — what THREE things could I cross off that would leave me feeling good about my productivity for the day?* (If your answer is nothing — your expectations are too high. A problem I have run into many times. Choose three anyway.) Mark these three items with a star. Tomorrow morning, review these priorities. If you finish them, you can progress to the other items on your list — but nothing else should come before these three priorities.

When completing your Before Snapshot on Day One, you rated your current satisfaction in a number of life areas. You also made a mark indicating where you would like to be. Look at the red lines that indicate your goals. Compare these goals with your starred-items. Does one of the starred-items help move you toward improving the highest area of desired change? For example, if money management is the problem, does your DAILY-ACTION list include at least one item to help improve that area of your life? If not, it's time for revision. Remove one of your starred items and replace it with something that will move you toward your goals.

This seems simple enough, but you would be amazed how many people will find that on most days, their DAILY-ACTION ITEMS have little to-do with their personal goals. We get bogged down with "this and that" and don't CHOOSE to make time for the areas that we know we need to change. We put everything else in front of change. Not anymore. Each day, make sure your DAILY ACTION ITEMS include one activity that moves you toward your highest snapshot goal. When you find yourself where you want to be in one area, move on to another area that needs improvement.

If you do not implement this part of the system, six months from now, you'll find yourself in the exact same place you are now. There is a great saying, "If you keep doing what you're doing, you'll keep getting what you're getting." Obviously — you don't want to "keep getting what you're getting" so try this new approach.

Most days you'll be able to easily cross off all three items and move on to other things — but on some days getting through the three items will be a chore. There are a few reasons for choosing just three DAILY-ACTION ITEMS:

1. To keep us focused and avoid spinning our wheels
2. To have a sense of accomplishment each day instead of feeling we didn't get enough done and/or having a load of guilt on our shoulders
3. Tackling three items isn't overwhelming — when we do ten or twenty or more, we can quickly burnout on the program

So put away the Super-Woman Cape and focus on three daily objectives. I guarantee you will get more done (and more of the RIGHT stuff done) than if you try to accomplish twenty daily tasks.

Your Assignment

Identify your three daily objectives, making sure they align with the goals from your Before Snapshot.

Day 8
Make a Pact with Your Self

✵

"Our real problem is not our strength today;
it is rather the vital necessity of action today
to ensure our strength tomorrow."
Calvin Coolidge

At this stage, "Challengers" are often developing confidence in prioritizing and internal change — while being eager to realize external change. In phase two we will begin taking control of the external, but before doing so we are going to make a pact together. Actually, I want you to be anxious to begin organizing — that is part of the plan! In this planning phase, we begin to anxiously anticipate change. While we anticipate, we think how wonderful it will be when our "physical" world is set to run smoothly. The more thought we put into change prior to actually changing, the better results we will have.

On the following page, you will find a pact. You'll notice that there is an area to list three reasons for why you are willing to make a commitment to the 70-Day Challenge. I hope the assignments we have embarked on together thus far have helped you identify your reasons for change.

Change Your Life Challenge Pact

I ______________________________ am willing to commit to the 70-Day Change Your Life Challenge because I want to experience life differently. Three of my specific motivations are:

1. ____

____

2. ____

____

3. ____

____

I commit to working through each daily challenge, regardless of how long it takes me.

____

Signature and Date

Don't jot down the first things that come to mind or skip the pact entirely. Remember, whenever you don't do the assignments as they are written you decrease your chances for success. You didn't embark on the 70-Day Make Your Life More Complicated Challenge — so try and follow the directions.

When I created this challenge for my own personal need I had many reasons to commit. Here are a few from my personal list:

I am tired of living on a perpetual treadmill.
I do a zillion things a day but I still don't have time for the things that really matter.
I am tired of not feeling great physically.
I want to take better care of myself.
I am tired of the "funks" I get when my house, personal life, or work life are in disarray.

Don't just copy what I have written. Personalize this — make it your own with reasons that really touch you. When you have completed the pact, make a copy for the front of your binder.

Your Assignment

Complete the pact, carefully considering each reason you choose.

✎ A copy of this pact is included in the workbook.

Day 9
How Effectively Do You Use Your Time?

✵

"There are those of us who are always about to live. We are waiting until things change, until there is more time, until we are less tired, until we get a promotion, until we settle down — until, until, until. It always seems as if there is some major event that must occur in our lives before we begin living."
George Sheehan

Any program that is devoted to life change can't work unless time is our friend and we utilize time to accomplish our goals.

Today we will cover some ideas for effective time management. Like all components of this program, the worst thing to do is to bite off more than you can chew. Instead of trying to implement all of these ideas at once, choose one to work with for a week. Once you are confident that item is incorporated, add another. Continue trying and testing ideas until you have created a customized time-management program that works for you. Research shows that it takes 30 days to develop a new habit, so remember to give your self some time.

FIVE- OR TEN-MINUTE TIME SPRINTS: We put off so much while waiting for the "perfect time," when so much of what we need to-do can be tackled in small increments. As you have likely realized the "perfect time" rarely comes. While life usually doesn't present large blocks of uninterrupted time, we regularly have five or ten minute segments. By having your CATCH-ALL notebook with you, you can quickly glance at your SHORT-TERM TO-DO items and find one that can be completed or partially completed, in a five- or ten-minute increment. Is there a phone call you could make? A thank you card you might write? While you may not be able to clean and remodel a kitchen in five or ten minutes, you could empty and reload a dishwasher, fold a load of laundry, or clean out a drawer. When we maximize the five or ten minute "breaks" in our lives, we take great strides toward effective time management and accomplishing our goals.

LARGE TIME BLOCKS: At one point in my life, when I wasn't as organized as I am now, I tried to schedule my time into concise increments, fifteen minutes, thirty minutes, *etc*. (Many calendars promote this thirty- to sixty-minute thinking with their detailed hours and minutes running down the left-hand column.) I found this approach to be very disappointing. I often over-estimated what I could accomplish and instead of feeling positive about what I had achieved, I felt discouraged by all the things I wanted to achieve but didn't get done. During that period, a pastor shared a TIME BLOCK system that he had used successfully. Here's how it works:

Break your day into major "time blocks." Here is an example of how my day would break into "blocks:"

5:30 to 9:00 Wake up, get Sammy ready for school

9:00 to 12:00 Before lunch
12:30 to 4:00 After Lunch
4:00 to 8:00 Sammy comes home, dinner prep, nightly routines
8:00 to12:00 All is quiet

Instead of trying to book my efforts in fifteen- to thirty-minute increments, Pastor Jeff encouraged me to write down the items I could accomplish during these "blocks" of time. With fifteen- to thirty-minute President-like scheduled tasks, an entire day can be disrupted if you do not stay perfectly on schedule. Whose life runs that smoothly? Jeff's time-block system offers more flexibility, making it easier to stay on schedule.

REVISIT THE DAILY-ACTION ITEMS: If you have not been using the DAILY-ACTION ITEMS go back and get reacquainted with that part of the program (see Day Seven). The Daily Action Items help us move forward each and every day by living in line with our priorities. For many, this alone will be the only time management tool that is needed.

CREATE A QUOTA: For those of you who say "yes" to everything, I strongly encourage the setting of a quota. Choose an amount of time that you feel comfortable devoting to outside activities. Make sure to consult your calendar so you choose a realistic amount of time. Don't choose an amount that will leave you stretched too thin and discouraged. Each week, when someone asks you to-do something "outside the norm," check and see if you have any "quota time" available. If yes, make sure that this endeavor is in alignment with your priorities and how you want to use your valuable time. If no, politely decline. If your "quota time" is five hours per week, and you reach that each and every week, be proud that you consistently give five hours, instead of feeling bad when you have to say "no" because the commitment would exceed quota.

THINK IN TERMS OF ROUTINES: We've all undoubtedly heard that children function best when following structure and routines. Getting things done (often things we don't really want to-do) is also easier when done by routine. Create a list of the commonly repeated duties and tasks you perform (or would/should perform) each day. Examples include preparing kids for school, preparing dinner and doing homework, preparing for bed, exercise, *etc.* Set a firm time to complete these items, and then list out their components. For example, when I wake each morning, I complete the following routine before my daughter wakes:

1. Say good morning to myself
2. Do a few minutes of stretching while visualizing my day going smoothly and effectively
3. Dress for the day
4. Have a cup of coffee while reviewing my to-do list or reading something uplifting

This can easily be done in twenty minutes because I have it down to a routine.

Taxed by To-Dos

If you are having a hard time taking control of your time, it could be as simple as a logistical impossibility. I have known many people who simply put too much on to-do lists. No matter what, they will never accomplish everything, because it *can't* be done. This is why the priority-planning exercise is so important. It forces us to focus. However, there are still those who will become frustrated and want to "do everything." Remember we can have it all, but not at the same time.

After the unexpected death of my twenty-seven-year-old brother, I finally understood the true gift and value of time. I was amazed at how so many things that had once seemed so important, became so trivial. How I wished I could turn back time and change where my focus had been, freeing up more time for living, sharing, loving. You can conduct a similar "reality check" by looking over the tasks that have filled your days over the past several months. Examine each day closely. Then ask yourself a very tough question: *If I were to die tomorrow, what on my calendar that seems so important — doesn't really matter? Where can I carve out more time for living? Sharing? Loving?*

This exercise along with a time log, can truly help us analyze our time and escape taxing to-do lists. A time log allows you to-document all your time over a designated period. I would suggest logging a week to start. Record everything that you do for a minimum of seven days. Then look back at your time log and ask yourself where you can find more time for living.

✎ Time log sheets can be found in the *Companion Workbook*.

Your Assignment

Choose one idea from today's reading to work with over the next few days, and then add another.

Day 10
A Prescription for Procrastination

"Know the true value of time; snatch, seize, and enjoy every moment of it. No idleness, no delay, no procrastination; never put off till tomorrow what you can do today."
Earl of Chesterfield

Today we will start with a quiz:

1. Do you have a CATCH-ALL notebook?	YES	NO
2. Have you created your CYLC Binder?	YES	NO
3. Have you done your Nightly Reflection more nights than you have NOT?	YES	NO
4. Did you paste a quote on the front of your Binder?	YES	NO
5. Have you completed the "Before Snapshot?"	YES	NO
6. Have you completed the CYLC Pact?	YES	NO
7. Have you been writing down your three DAILY-ACTION ITEMS?	YES	NO
8. Have you been completing your DAILY-ACTION ITEMS?	YES	NO

Give yourself one point for each YES answer.

Let's see how you did.

8 to 10 Way to go! You are on the right track. You probably won't hit many procrastination pitfalls in this program.

5 to 7 You are in the middle-ground. You are doing well for making so many changes so quickly in spite of your busy life. You could easily go either way — really commit to the program or fade out. What will you choose?

0 to 4 This day is for you. We need to have a talk about procrastination.

Procrastination: THE CAUSE

Since you are a procrastinator and might procrastinate reading this, I am going to try to get right to the point. Procrastination always has an underlying cause — usually an emotional one. Read through the list below and try to honestly assess why you procrastinate. Circle the statements that apply to you — and please, don't procrastinate your circling!

1. You don't really want to get organized.
2. Getting organized would cause you to face the disorganized areas in your life, which you would rather just "sweep" under the rug.
3. You are fatigued or depressed.

4. You enjoy living an unfulfilled life and wouldn't know what to-do with yourself if you had extra hours on your hands or peace in your heart. You are "addicted to chaos."
5. You've tried so many things you are concerned you will just end up with another plan that doesn't work.
6. You haven't clearly defined your goals or done your worksheets so you can't clearly envision the benefits you will achieve.
7. You are missing some information or there is something you do not understand.
8. You are over-committed — trying to-do so much at one time that you are "freezing" yourself still.
9. You are a perfectionist and because you always want to achieve an impossible standard you never get started.
10. You are waiting for the right time to begin.

If you followed the instructions, you have circled the statements that apply to your situation. These are the reasons behind your inaction. Let's see what action steps we can take to make forward progress.

Procrastination: THE CURE

1. You don't really want to get organized or lack commitment.

I don't mean to sound harsh but this is an easy one: You aren't ready to accept this challenge yet and should close the book. Although you like the idea of change, you aren't ready to take the action. Perhaps you haven't hit your "breaking point." Ideally, we implement a program prior to reaching that stressful place, but sometimes we have to "go into the darkness" to realize how much we need to change our life. Try again when you are ready to commit, otherwise you are just going to get frustrated, not feel good about the program, and perhaps damage your self-esteem.

2. ***Getting organized would cause you to face the disorganized areas of your life, which you would rather just "sweep" under the rug.***

Divide a piece of paper into two columns; label one "PROS" and the other "CONS." Write down what unpleasant areas you will have to face as part of this challenge under the CONS column. Write down the PROS of having a complete life-makeover and organized life in the other. Which side will you choose as your reality?

✏ A pro and con worksheet can be found in the *Companion Workbook.*

3. You are fatigued or depressed.

It is perfectly okay to have an "off day" and to take a day off from the program. The problem arises when days turn into weeks. First, evaluate why you are tired and/or depressed. Do you need to talk to someone? Is your fatigue or depression related to hormones or something else that might pass? If it is a chronic problem, seek help. If it is diet/exercise related, start adding diet items to your DAILY ACTION LIST. Take a baby step each day. Maybe you won't have the energy to go at the 70-day pace. That's okay. The key is to take SOME ACTION each day. You want to have CONSISTENT efforts.

4. You enjoy living an unfulfilled life and wouldn't know what to do with yourself if you had extra hours on your hands or peace in your heart. You are "addicted to chaos."

Then you are on the right track to maintaining your chaotic life. You will not commit to change because you find joy in chaos. This isn't a judgment; there are many people like this. Perhaps at a different phase of your life, you will desire a more-balanced lifestyle. Put this book away for when that day comes.

5. You've tried so many things you are concerned you will just end up with another plan that doesn't work.

Will seventy more days really hurt? Come on — give it a try. You have made it to Day Ten. Check out the Change Your Life Challenge Web Site (www.changeyourlifechallenge.com) for extra support. Consider purchasing the *Change Your Life Challenge Workbook* for further guidance.

6. You haven't clearly defined your goals or done your worksheets so you can't clearly envision the benefits you will achieve.

If someone told you to jump up and down for five hours, would you do it? My guess is that to even consider it, you would want to know what the reward would be at the end. If the reward meant enough, you might find yourself hopping! It's easy to procrastinate or put something off when we don't understand why we are doing it. You need to clearly visualize your goals. Try them on and see how they feel. Try closing your eyes for fifteen minutes and picturing a day living an effective, complete, fulfilling, well-balanced life. How do you feel? Are you eating healthier? Exercising? Have you made more time for kids and friends? Are relationships improving? Are your finances under control for the first time in a long while? Can you buy something without guilt because you have a designated "extra" fund? Is your house clean and organized? Is having a family dinner easier now that you have your meal planning done? Go ahead and make the challenge real for yourself by envisioning your goals. Try reflecting on this "new you" a few minutes each day for increased motivation.

✎ Complete the "New You" worksheet in the *Companion Workbook.*

7. You are missing some information or there is something you do not understand.

Sign onto the Change Your Life Challenge support board and ask. Don't let this be the excuse that keeps you from your life makeover.

8. You are over-committed — trying to-do so much at one time that you are "freezing" yourself still.

This is the one that usually gets me! I surround myself with so much to-do that I can't move. I used to be an extremist. If I couldn't do it all, I just wouldn't do anything. The only way to conquer was is to handle change in measured increments — thus the birth of the 70-Day Challenge. If you do just the day's work and don't add to it, make it more complicated, or skip ahead — this program should help to alleviate this procrastination pitfall.

9. You are a perfectionist and because you always want to meet an impossible standard you never get started.

Perfectionism will only lead to unhappiness because no one is perfect. Do you want to hold yourself to unreal standards for the rest of your life or do you want to join the human race? I was one of the WORST perfectionists. Eventually, I realized that attempts to be perfect at everything led to a lot of failure and poor self-esteem. You can keep running on the perfectionist treadmill, but know there isn't an exit where you will step off and be perfect.

10. You are waiting for the right time to start.

With all the conditions we put on "right," there will never be a "right time" unless we make one. We make time *now* for what is important. Take control of your time instead of letting it control you. The "right" time is now, today, this minute.

Your Assignment

Identify any reasons you procrastinate. Write down these obstacles and make a plan for rising above them. Share your ideas with your challenge partner. Hold each other accountable.

Day 11
The Family Message Board

✵

"No man is fit to command another
that cannot command himself."
William Penn

One of the items on the "Setting Up Shop" list was a dry-erase calendar board with cork. Today, you'll be hanging that board in a central location of your home. You will also need one dry-erase marker for each family member (a different color for each). You can attach a small bag or magnetic holder to the board to store the markers (or you may want to consider hanging them with a string if they tend to "walk away").

This calendar is the centralized area by which your family members should learn to communicate. Let each family member, age ten or older, be responsible for recording their plans and appointments on the board. For example, if a child brings home a note about a field trip, teach him to write the date with his color pen on the board. If a child has a sleepover or needs a ride to a friend's house, have her write this on the calendar. This provides a central area for you to view commitments of other family members that may affect you. If you have a partner that travels a lot or frequently works late, ask him to record his travel schedule, meetings, or late nights on the board, so you can plan for meals. I also recommend writing your own meetings and events on the board to allow family members to know where you will be and to anticipate planning conflicts.

I think it's important for kids to have the responsibility and accountability that comes with planning events to avoid last minute surprises for mom or dad. If they really want to-do something, they should be able to record it on the board. Let kids know that if it isn't on the board, it will not be planned for, and you cannot guarantee they will get to go. This simple talk will get everyone using the system quickly.

The cork side of the message board is for exchanging messages and vital information. For example, if your child has a permission slip for you to sign, he would post it on the cork side of the message board.

Our goal with the message board and the phone log (covered tomorrow) is to begin creating a centralized area for paper and communication so it doesn't fall through the cracks in today's busy world.

Your Assignment

Hang your message board in a high-traffic area. Inform family members of its purpose and how it should be used.

Day 12

The Master Phone Log

✵

"The control center of your life is your attitude."
Anonymous

This is the perfect time to put your spiral-bound phone-message log to work. I recommend the carbon version because then one copy of the message can stay in the book at all times. I can't tell you how many times it has proven handy to be able to flip back and find a message or a phone number.

Setting up a master phone log and phone binder might seem tedious since you already have a CONTACTS section in your CYLC Binder. I once thought that, too. I developed the master phone log after the CYLC Binder did not work for this function. What happened was that family members would need a phone number and either rummage through my CYLC Binder, or use the excuse of not knowing a number as a reason not to complete a task.

This centralized-master phone log, creates a known source where family members can find information to help maintain the household. If you live alone, or with just one other person, you may be able to get by using your CYLC Binder. In all other circumstances, I recommend this phone log.

Teach children how to take a message. You may even want to put a small prompter by the phone that reminds them to ask the name, phone number, what the message is regarding, and a good time to return the call. After taking a message, let family members know to tack the top copy on the message board, and to leave the other in the spiral bound book.

Next, we will make a master family phone book. Use the half-inch ring binder you purchase in the Setting Up Shop section. Sort this book by either adding alphabetical tabs, or by adding one tab per family member. Insert a couple of pocket folders onto the rings. These folders will be used for coupons or paperwork that matches the phone numbers.

This phone log is your "frequent call" list for the family. You do not need to put addresses in here. I keep my CONTACTS separate in my master CYLC Binder and use this for all the places that we all call on a regular basis. I also put coupons in a pocket folder. For example, I have the local pizza parlors listed in the book and then their coupons in a folder in the front. I have a coupon for a free oil change, so the next time I need to call for an oil change, I will remember to use the coupon.

For my daughter's friends, I write down both the child and her parents' names. If there are other kids in the family, I write down these names, too. This way I don't have to call and ask for "Taylor's Mom."

Basically, your goal with the centralized phone book is to provide easy access for OTHER family members to make calls and appointments. It keeps them from rummaging through your CYLC Binder and asking for numbers. You may want to tuck some sticky-notes in the inside pocket so when family members are looking for a number they can jot it down and take it with them instead of taking the whole binder.

The first page should have all your emergency phone numbers, fire number, and contact information.

Be prepared for a few ups and downs as you get the family system rolling. It takes 21 days to form a new habit and during those days there are bound to be some bumps along the way — but once implemented, this is a vital tool in a smooth running family system.

Your Assignment

Put together a master phone book for your home and let family members know where it is and how to use it. Explain the phone message log as well. Accuracy and attention to detail are key here.

The *Companion Workbook* contains a few other worksheets you may want to print and implement at this time, including the Birthday Book and the Prescription Pages.

Intermission: Attitudes and Gratitude

"Gratitude turns denial into acceptance, chaos to order, confusion to clarity. It can turn a meal into a feast, a house into a home, a stranger into a friend. Gratitude makes sense of our past, brings peace for today, and creates a vision for tomorrow."

Melody Beattie

Once with a group of women, we were discussing why it is that some children who seem to "have it all" are pleasant and friendly while others become spoiled. After sharing our stories, we drew the conclusion that the difference rests in the attitude and teachings of the parents. Some children "expect" to have certain things, and they soon become spoiled and unwavering. Other children remain thankful and appreciative.

Think of adults you know that fit these descriptions. Whom do you know who has a chip on their shoulder or feels the world owes them something? Whom do you know who greets each discovery with appreciation? It is easy to guess who is happier and more fulfilled.

Developing a thankful attitude, goes a long way toward developing a more resilient and appreciative self. Here are a few ideas for spreading the attitude of gratitude.

Think about the whole process. When you receive anything, be it a child's drawing or an expensive purchased gift, focus on how much time, effort, and thought went into the gift. Taking the time to realize how much work, caring, and thought a person has given you is a wonderful way to deepen your appreciation of both the giver and the gift.

Realize each day is a gift. There are so many things that we take for granted. Many times we don't realize how much we actually take for granted until tragedy strikes. For example, I always enjoyed my brother and never imagined we would lose him at age 27. It wasn't until after this tragedy that I learned each day and each moment we have is a precious gift. Don't be wasteful or unappreciative of these moments.

Lower your expectations. I knew a woman who felt that she had such a series of bad luck that the world surely owed her something. I couldn't stand being around her; she complained about everything. If it rained, it seemed the sky was out to get her.

When we quit expecting the world (or people) to give us things, we can become more focused on enjoying the gifts that do come our way.

Sarah Ban Breathnach in her best-selling book, *Simple Abundance: A Daybook of Comfort and Joy*, advocates the use of a gratitude journal. She sites this as "a tool that could change the quality of your life beyond belief." I completely agree. The premise of the gratitude journal is to record five things that you are grateful for each day. Some days you might have to be creative to find five. Other days you might have ten or twenty! Value the little things. Value the person who sincerely smiled and asked how you were at the grocery store checkout. Value the soft touch of a child's hand on your shoulder. Value a new song that you hear on the radio.

Create your own gratitude journal and list five things that you are grateful for each evening. Notice how this deepens your appreciation for life and helps to maintain a positive outlook. You may also want to start a "Family Gratitude Journal" where each night you think of five things that you are grateful for as a family.

Part Two
The Nitty-Gritty

✵

Dealing With the In-House, Disorganized Backlog

Daily Routine Action List

Days Thirteen through Fifteen:

- ☐ Complete your gratitude journal each evening.
- ☐ Begin each day with a heartfelt "good morning."
- ☐ Carry your CATCH-ALL notebook with you everywhere.
- ☐ Transfer your to-do list each night.
- ☐ Complete your Nightly Reflection each evening.
- ☐ Each day, use the three-step action list.

Days Sixteen through Nineteen:

- ☐ Complete your gratitude journal each evening.
- ☐ Begin each day with a heartfelt "good morning."
- ☐ Carry your CATCH-ALL notebook with you everywhere.
- ☐ Transfer your to-do list each night.
- ☐ Complete your Nightly Reflection each evening.
- ☐ Each day, use the three-step action list.
- ☐ Consult your MASTER TASK LISTS for any other tasks that need to be completed.

Days Twenty through 37:

- ☐ Complete your gratitude journal each evening.
- ☐ Begin each day with a heartfelt "good morning."
- ☐ Carry your CATCH-ALL notebook with you everywhere.
- ☐ Transfer your to-do list each night.
- ☐ Complete your Nightly Reflection each evening.
- ☐ Each day, use the three-step action list.
- ☐ Consult your MASTER TASK LISTS for any other tasks that need to be completed.
- ☐ Do a daily laundry load if volume warrants.

Day 13

Preparing for Our First Mission

"Failing to plan means planning to fail.
Brian Tracy

Now that you have the basics of your CATCH-ALL notebook down and we have covered some internal change factors, we are going to shift gears. We are going to roll up our sleeves and get to the actual organization within our home. The first step is easy: preparation.

Four Rubber-Maid® or other large plastic containers
Two large cardboard boxes
Lined paper
Tape
Pen

Label your containers as follows:

Cardboard Box #1 - THROW AWAY

Cardboard Box #2 - GIVE AWAY

Plastic Container # 1 - STOW AWAY

Plastic Container # 2 - PUT AWAY

Plastic Container # 3 - STORE AWAY

Plastic Container # 4 - SELL

(You could use cardboard boxes for everything. I personally like the plastic containers because they are easy to haul with the handles. They also stack nicely and keep items safe from moisture.)

This part of the program is similar to many organizing systems, but I have added a twist or two. Since I am one of those people who have a hard time throwing anything away, I can appreciate the fear that runs up and down a person's spine at the thought of throwing out something. Maybe it's in the genes. My grandmother once had a fit when I tried to throw away a bunch of half-squirrel-eaten Indian corn.

"Not the Indian corn," she screamed. I had never seen an 87-year-old woman sprint before, but she was determined to rescue the corn! In any event, since I am sympathetic to the clutter-bug gene, I've tried to modify the typical clean-and-clear program with a special STOW AWAY box.

Also, many organizing systems I have tried suggested only four boxes: SELL, GIVE, TRASH, DECIDE LATER. I found that I had to re-sort countless times. I've made six boxes in this system to help get the items into the right place once and for all. Let's look at each of your boxes in detail.

THROW AWAY: I won't offer much explanation on this one. The more you can put into these boxes, the simpler your life will become. As we all know, "stuff" uses energy. The less stuff you have, the less energy you expend taking care of it (dusting it, washing it, fixing it, *etc.*) and the more space you create for stress-free living.

***NOTE TO SERIOUS CLUTTER-BUGS:** If you skimmed over the last paragraph because the thought of throwing something away leaves you nauseous, try the following: Choose one room of your house to be your spacious room. Simplify the room as much as possible. You don't have to throw anything away — just move it. Note how different the room feels with the newfound space. This might inspire you to de-clutter other areas of your life!*

GIVE AWAY: Start by taping a piece of paper to this box. Anything that you are going to give to a charity, church, or others should go in this box. Write each item on your piece paper as you put it in the box. When you get to the point of taking the box to the donation drop off, present your piece of paper as an itemized receipt of the contents. The organization can sign your paper or give you another receipt for your tax deduction.

PUT AWAY: Undoubtedly as we move through our homes we will find many things that are in the wrong place. Perhaps we were too busy and never gave a new item the "proper home" or perhaps Junior has a habit of bringing every toy into the kitchen and now you have plastic army men in your muffin-tin cups. Whatever the item, place it in the PUT AWAY box. If your home has a lot of stuff in the wrong place, consider making a couple of PUT AWAY boxes, maybe one for upstairs and one for downstairs.

STORE AWAY: As you go through this program you may discover seasonal or infrequently used items that are taking up valuable space. Reclaim that space by carefully storing the items into boxes and then placing them in a garage, basement, or closet. Make sure to label each box clearly for easy recognition. I like to use the same size paper or stickers so that all the labels are consistent. It makes it very easy to scan the boxes for just what you need. Sticking a piece of paper to this box, just as we did for the giveaway box, can serve as an easy way to inventory its contents.

SELL: Anything you choose to sell goes into this box. However, there are a few sale rules. If you plan on having a garage sale you must have it within 120 days. No HOARDING items for years while waiting for the perfect garage-sale day. Trust me — there isn't one.

After moving from Milwaukee to Portland, and back again I was amazed that I had amassed ten boxes of inexpensive trinkets for a garage sale. Six years had passed since I intended to have my garage sale and my back seriously regretted the decision to crate these boxes back and forth across the country. Had I just donated or thrown away the items I would have saved time and energy.

There are other ways of selling besides garage sales. In Portland we had a great clothing consignment store. You could take in up to thirty items per month. Each month as you brought in new items, they issued a check for what had sold the previous month. Check the Yellow Pages for consignment shops in your neighborhood.

I have also fallen in love with E-Bay. Selling through E-bay is simple and efficient. If you have a digital camera, a bank account, and an email address you can get started in a flash. If you don't have a digital camera, take photos of your items with a regular camera but ask your photo development location to put the pictures on disk. It only takes an hour or two to learn how to use E-Bay and it is a great way to sell items valued at $12 or more. (You can sell lower price items but I have found that with the listing fee and time involved $12 is the lowest I like to go. Try it yourself and set your own "low-limit.")

STOW AWAY: The stow away box is for all the items that give you a headache when trying to decide which box to put them in. Instead of huffing, puffing, and blowing up in frustration, put them in the STOW AWAY box. Make sure to tape a piece of your ruled paper to this box and write down what you stow. The one rule I have for STOWING is to revisit each of the stowed boxes within four to six months. Often when we look at these items fresh, we can easily decide whether to give them away, sell them, junk them, store them or re-stow them. Thin your STOW AWAY boxes regularly.

Your Assignment

Get your boxes and containers together and labeled so you are ready to declutter.

Day 14
Tackling the Bathroom

✵

"There are no menial jobs, only menial attitudes."
William John Bennett

I realize that starting our cleaning expedition in the bathroom probably doesn't sound exciting, but being it's a small room, it makes sense to start here. You can learn basic organizing skills quickly and see progress right away. We will then take the skills and expand them as we tackle closets, kids rooms, *etc.*, until we've gone through the entire house.

Go ahead and take your six containers into a bathroom. Take this book along with your CATCH-ALL notebook. Also, since you are staying in your home, your CYLC Binder gets to go on a field trip. Take it with you as you begin today's assignment.

Step One: Round Up the Washables

Go ahead and grab everything that is washable — rugs, towels, *etc.*, and throw them in the washer while you complete this process. Don't bother to put out new towels, instead replace the towels when they are clean. This is principle one: Multi-task. This simple step avoids creating a laundry heap that becomes another stressful "thing that needs to be done."

Step Two: Peek Under the Sink

Assuming you have an "under-the-sink," take everything out and place it on the floor. If your bathroom is anything like mine you'll have a garbage can and miscellaneous odd things that need a home. Go ahead and sort each item into one of your six containers. Empty your garbage and then put extra garbage bags at the bottom before placing in a new liner. This way when you empty your garbage you will have a fresh liner waiting for you. Toss the garbage in your trash box.

Step Three: Make a Cleaning Station

Find a small box, caddy, or plastic container. In this container you are going to put everything you need to clean your bathroom. This would include glass cleaner, paper towels or rags, a scrub brush, toilet and tile cleaners, a small sweep broom, floor cleaner, and any other supplies you need. You will create one of these cleaning stations for each bathroom. It may seem like overkill but often when we have extra minutes, we don't clean because we don't have the items handy. For example, if you are drawing bathwater you can easily spray down the mirror or counters while waiting. Also, doing a little bit here and there avoids a nasty, messy pile up. Don't worry about how often you do these things at this point — we will cover that when we create your master plan. For now, we just want to set the stage for success.

Step Four: Start Your Master Supply List

Turn to the tab marked SHOPPING LISTS in your CYLC Binder. Write BATHROOM at the top of a blank piece of paper. Write down all the items in your cleaning caddy on this sheet of paper. This is the beginning of your MASTER HOUSEHOLD SHOPPING LIST. Eventually you will have a full MASTER LIST that includes every item needed to maintain your home. You will use that list to easily check "stock" before shopping.

Today you will be making two lists: (1) A list in your MASTER BINDER that shows everything needed for bathroom maintenance; (2) A list in your CATCH-ALL notebook of those items you need to purchase to get your cleaning stations up and running (this list would go on your SHORT-TERM TO-DO page). For example, if you have one bottle of glass cleaner but two bathrooms, write down that you need a second bottle of glass cleaner. I realize that household supplies are expensive so there is a bit of cost incurred in setting up these stations — however consider it an investment in your sanity. You are worth it and it will make cleaning so much easier. Also watch the Sunday paper. Most cleaning supplies have coupons and when you purchase them at a store like Wal-Mart or K-Mart with a coupon, you can get a great price. Dollar-stores also frequently have inexpensive cleaning supplies. Or you can purchase one large container and then divvy it up into smaller spray bottles for each cleaning station. One addition I made to my "Bathroom Caddy" was a small dustpan and broom (the hand-held kind). I found these for $1.99 and bought a few of them. I have placed them near small, uncarpeted floors or stairs so I can sweep in a flash without having to find my big broom (which seems to love playing hide and seek).

A key to successful household maintenance involves having the needed supplies at your fingertips when you have the time to use them. When you have the items near you, then you can easily use your five-minute segments to clean, versus spending the five minutes looking for the items you need.

Step Five: Use Your Caddy

Use your Cleaning Caddy to clean your bathroom. Are there any other items you need or have missed? Sometimes as we complete the actual cleaning additional list items become apparent. If you have a big bathroom or one that hasn't been cleaned in a while, break it down. Just be careful not to procrastinate, you should be taking SOME action daily. Anything you don't accomplish today should be recorded on the SHORT-TERM TO-DO list.

Step Six: Go Through the Medicine Cabinet

Assuming you have a medicine cabinet, take the time to go through its contents. Check prescriptions and expiration dates and throw out any old items. Throw out any old lotions, bottles, or miscellaneous beauty supplies that have gone in and out of vogue since you owned them. Use the same technique for your drawers, using the six containers as necessary. If you have drawers filled with makeup you can leave those for now — we will tackle makeup and handbags separately. Add any items you discover that are used regularly to your MASTER SHOPPING LIST (*i.e.*, toothpaste, Band-Aids®, aspirin, shaving cream).

Step Seven: Write Down What You Did

Turn to the MASTER TASK LIST tab of your CYLC Binder. Write down the different things that you have done (or need to-do) in the bathroom. Here is a sampling of what you may want to include:

BATHROOM DUTIES
Go through medicine cabinet
Clean beneath sink
Clean and sort through drawers
Sweep floor
Mop floor
Clean bathtub
Do bathroom laundry
Clean toilet
Wipe down mirrors
Wipe down counters

✎ I have included my complete list for each room in the *Companion Workbook* as a springboard.

If you have more than one bathroom, write down a list for each bathroom. The lists could be different; you may not have bathtubs in both bathrooms. Label each list applicably — MASTER BATH, UPSTAIRS BATH, HALF BATH — or whatever heading will allow you to remember which list is for which bathroom.

Step Eight: Put Your Towels in the Dryer

Transfer bathroom wash into the dryer. Don't do as I used to and forget about it, leaving it to live long enough in the washer that it takes on a life of its own.

Step Nine: Go Through Your Containers

Take your THROW AWAY box to the garbage if it is full, otherwise move it to the next bathroom or room you will be doing. Take your GIVE AWAY box and tape it closed (if full). Tape your list of contents to the top. Put it in the car to take to your local charity the next time you have a minute. Take your STOW AWAY box and seal it with the contents list on top — then stow it. You probably don't have anything in your STORE AWAY box so just move it to the next room. Inventory the contents of your SELL box and then give yourself a deadline for selling it. Make the deadline within the next ninety days. If you don't sell these items by then, give them away. Make sure to write the sale deadline on your SHORT-TERM or LONG-TERM TO-DO list.

Step Ten: Go Get Your Laundry!

Go grab your towels out of the dryer and hang them back up. Fluff your rugs and give yourself a pat on the back for accomplishing Mission One.

Repeat the process with each bathroom. If you get the jitters tackling this, break it down. Commit to working on it for fifteen minutes in the morning and fifteen minutes each night. Before you know it, you'll be looking back wondering why you hadn't done this sooner!

Your Assignment

Use the steps from today to tackle (or begin tackling) your first bathroom.

Day 15
Exploring the Master Task List

✵

"Continuous effort — not strength or intelligence — is the key to unlocking our potential."
Winston Churchill

At some point in the past fourteen days, you have likely pondered how we are going to manage the many daily and weekly to-dos that never go away — like laundry, doing the dishes, cleaning jobs, *etc.* That's the topic of today's challenge. We will be creating a master schedule that will be kept in your CYLC Binder. Locate the list we created yesterday of bathroom cleaning duties. Behind the MASTER TASK LIST tab of your binder, add some loose-leaf paper.

Choose any room to begin with. Go into the room and explore it as if seeing it for the first time. What do you need to-do to maintain the room? It doesn't matter if these things are done daily or monthly or yearly — just write them all down. Work through each room on a separate sheet of paper, labeling the paper with the room type, *i.e.*, kitchen, living room, den, bedroom.

✎ A sample list for each room is included in the *Companion Workbook.*

IMPORTANT: *Make sure to break down the tasks! Don't write CLEAN APPLIANCES — instead list out each appliance. Don't put CLEAN FLOORS— instead list out each task you do — sweep, mop, wax, etc.*

Continue doing this for each room of the house until you have everything written down. Tomorrow we will be moving this list onto a master schedule. If you have a large house or your list-making takes several days, just stop the CYCL Challenge and pick it up when you have your lists completed. No one is going to mind if you have a seventy-three day challenge.

Your Assignment

Complete the "task/cleaning" inventory of each room in your house.

Day 16
Working With Your Master Task List

✵

"It is our attitude at the beginning of a difficult task
which, more than anything else,
will affect its successful outcome."
William James

Grab yesterday's assignment, as we will be referring to those task lists quite a bit today. If you haven't completed Day 15, you will need to before continuing with today's assignment.

Today you will really begin to see some "system programming" as we think through all of our to-dos. Don't worry about how you will ever accomplish everything on your list. Now is not the time to concern yourself with these things. We will deal with that a bit later. For now, just focus on the directions that follow.

Grab the task lists you made on Day 15.

There are two worksheets you will need for today. Before beginning, let's look at the purpose of each worksheet. (You will find both of these worksheets in the Appendix and in the *Companion Workbook.*)

Monthly Task List: This worksheet has columns numbered one through 31. You will be using this worksheet to organize tasks that are done at least every other week. You will need two to three copies of the Monthly Task List worksheet for each month, depending on how many tasks you have.

Yearly Task List: This worksheet has a column for each month of the year. You will be using this worksheet to organize tasks that are done once a month or less. You will need one or two copies of this worksheet, depending on how many tasks you have.

Work through each task from your Day Fifteen assignment, and place it on one of these two worksheets. If the task is done more frequently than once per month, place it on the Monthly Task List. On the Monthly Task List, the columns represent the days of the month. Place an X on the days you will perform the task based on how frequently it needs to be done. I like to categorize my tasks by ROOM on the worksheets. For the kitchen, I might list the following entries:

Empty and load dishwasher: This is a task I perform daily, so I would put an X in every column on the Monthly Task List.

Sweep Floor: I like to-do this twice a week in the kitchen. Since I am working on my June plan, I would consult a calendar and place an X under whichever two days I choose on the Monthly Task List.

Defrost Freezer: I do this twice a year (if I'm lucky). Since it is not done monthly I would write this item on the Yearly Task List and then check the month (or months) I plan to complete it. For example, I'll pick December and next May as my two months for defrosting the freezer. I'll then place an X on the Yearly Task List in each of those columns. In summary, if the task is one you would do twice a year, place an X under two months you plan to complete the task. If you would complete the task three times per year, place an X under three months of your choice.

Are You with Me so Far?

We are creating a log for all the maintenance components of our life. Why? Because when we are stressed or depressed, it usually isn't the "major" issues life brings, but a piling-up of the "little things." These Master Task worksheets allow us to control our daily and monthly tasks, instead of the other way around.

These worksheets allow us to take a quick glance and capture all that is going on in our lives and what we need to-do in any given day. Don't do all the months yet — just do your first full month and then your yearly worksheet. I recommend working in pencil in case you need to alter your plan, or other parts of this challenge alter your way of looking at tasks.

Let's take a moment to reflect on your completed worksheets and see if we can't simplify them a bit to create more time for you.

1. Look at your recorded tasks. Find five things that really don't matter much to you and DECREASE the frequency of how often you do them. Are there any other tasks that you could do less frequently? Are there any tasks you could eliminate altogether?

2. Is there anything on your list that someone else can do? Do you have kids who should/could be doing chores? We are covering Chore and Reward Systems later in the challenge. For now look at which tasks could be completed by another family member. If your significant other isn't pulling his weight, mark the tasks you need help with and write his name in the "task manager" column. Review the list with your significant other and ask for help. See if there are any tasks you are doing more often than needed because you feel it is important to your significant other, when he really doesn't mind if it is done less frequently. If you have a demanding partner and you can't eliminate much or he will not help, then know that you will have to let some things slide here and there. Try alternating which things you focus on so nothing gets completely out of hand.

IMPORTANT: *Before you decide that your significant other won't help or that you must do everything regularly — ASK! Don't just assume. Make sure to have a conversation about it. Many people have been convinced that they could not get help from another family member, only to have very different results after a heart-to-heart (non-blaming) conversation.*

---

3. Is your plan realistic? Make sure you aren't setting an unrealistic schedule for yourself. Does everything need to be done as often as you have scheduled? You don't want to be a slob of course, however you don't want to obsess and overwork yourself if the task isn't very important to your family. Remember that each task takes away from your self-time, time to spend with family members, on work, or in service to the community. Decide what your own personal standard is and then make sure your task schedule matches. For example, some people dust every week. When my family discussed our task list, we decided that board games were more fun! Instead of spending our time dusting, we spend time playing games and dust every five to six weeks. (When my edits came back on this book, the copy editor had written in red pen, *five to six weeks without dusting is too long*. She suggested I replace it with *three or four weeks.* I didn't. This is a good example of how someone else might have a different standard. For my family, and me five to six weeks is just fine.)

4. Remember that some tasks are easier the more often they are done. If you leave shower cleaner in the tub and spray after each shower, you will not end up with a "clean shower/tub task" that takes two hours. If you don't periodically maintain the shower, then it will be labor-intensive and difficult.

At this point you should have all your tasks transferred to your MASTER TASK LIST and have analyzed them to some degree. If the list is messy due to changes or adjustments, go ahead and rewrite. Now, when the next full month starts, try and follow your chart. I like to put a circle around each X when the task is completed.

Don't worry if you don't get through everything. We will be evaluating your progress with this MASTER TASK LIST later and can make adjustments as necessary.

As each new month starts, consult the Yearly Task List for any of your infrequent tasks that are due to be done that month. Add them to your list that is broken down by day and place an X under the day it will be done. Also, don't be intimidated by your tasks! If you find you are avoiding something either break it down into easier steps or make it your first thing to tackle on a given day to just get it over with. If you are avoiding a task repeatedly this is a red light that it is either not a priority for you or it is just too big and needs to be broken down into accomplishable steps.

It may take a few days to adjust and organize your task list. Again, don't obsess about how you are going to get everything done. Just try it. Take it day by day. *Plan a month at a time, but work and focus a DAY at a time.*

Lastly — place these lists in the MASTER TASK LIST section of your CYLC Binder. As you do your planning and reflection each night, you can move any needed items over to your CATCH-ALL notebook.

Your Assignment

Print and complete your master task worksheets. Put them in your Change Your Life Challenge Binder. Begin incorporating your daily task list into your nightly reflection by writing any tasks you must complete on your SHORT-TERM page of your CATCH-ALL notebook.

Day 17
Conquering Your Closet

✵

"I have found that if you love life,
life will love you back."
Arthur Rubinstein

Reading the "C" word may make you recoil in horror. Needless to say, this challenge isn't for those who lack courage or for the faint of heart. Going boldly doesn't entail conquering just the junk drawer. In the *Change Your Life Challenge* we go for the gusto, the big time, the whole enchilada. That being said, you don't have to tackle your whole closet in a day! We will take simple steps each day to tackle this big job. As a Chinese Proverb states, "yard by yard life is hard ... inch by inch, it's a cinch."

So my guess is you have more than one of these "C-word" areas in your home. The good news is that you can pretend (for now) that you only have one. Yours. We will be practicing our simplifying principles and using our six containers in the closet starting tomorrow. First we need to-do some prep work.

1. Grab all of your dirty clothes and clean them. This also includes dry cleaning. (Imagine my surprise when I found all my missing kitchen towels and long-lost summer shorts underneath my many, varied piles.)

2. **Take anything that is off-season, fold it neatly, and pack it away in a labeled STOW AWAY container.** I like those large plastic Rubbermaid containers. They can be stacked easily in a garage, attic or another "C-word" area.

3. **Move all your dress clothes or any fancy-wear that you don't use often into a hard-to-reach area of your closet.** Most people have a foot of "non-prime" closet space. Use this to hang the items you rarely use. If all your closet space is prime (you're lucky) just put infrequently worn items at the end of one of the closet rods.

BEFORE AND AFTER CONTEST

I would love to see before and after photos of your closet. Twice a year we will be awarding a Rush Hour Library (includes 12 books on various aspects of time and life management) to our "after winner"). To enter, simply take a BEFORE photo, then complete the steps in this assignment and take an AFTER photo. Send both photos along with your name and contact information to Champion Press, Ltd., Before and After Contest, 4308 Blueberry Road, Fredonia WI 53021. We cannot accept electronic submissions. Winners will be announced on the CYLC web site and their photographs will be posted.

---

4. Grab a box and remove all the hangers from your closet that don't have clothes on them.

5. Now arrange all your hangers so that they are facing the same direction. This will help avoid tangles that require advanced yoga-skills in order to excavate yourself.

Your closet preparation is done. You will be ready to go when we dig in tomorrow. If you found that was easier than you thought and you have extra time leftover, feel free to go on to another closet.

Your Assignment

Complete the Pre-Closet steps outlined today.

Day 18
Digging in the Closet Depths

✵

"Keep your face to the sunshine
and you cannot see the shadow."
Helen Adams Keller

If you have completed the pre-closet work from yesterday you are ready to dig into the depths of your closet. Don't be scared. Again, breaking this into manageable tasks will make it a breeze.

1. Decide what is going to be on hangers and what is going to be stacked. Are you going to hang sweaters or fold them? What about tee-shirts and light cottons? Pants? I love to hang just about everything to decrease wrinkles. (I don't own an iron.) Excluding my sweaters, I hang everything else. While thinking about this, consider the hanging rods in your closet "prime real estate." This is where you want to hang the items you wear the most. If you are short on hanging space, consider adding another rod so your closet has two rods across.

Even though I love to hang my clothes, I did go through a season of life where I never had the time to hang anything. Instead I became a "piler." I quickly adapted my system by putting a bunch of crates into my closet. Then when I folded laundry I could just transfer the pile into a crate and didn't have to worry about piles on the floor that were waiting to be "hung."

2. Now that you have decided, go ahead and put everything in its proper place. If you need more hangers, go out and grab some. Hang like items together. I put all my long-sleeve cotton shirts together, then my long sleeve blouses, then turtlenecks, then tee-shirts, then blazers and work clothes, then skirts, *etc.* If it's hot out and I want a tee-shirt, I know exactly where to look.

3. At this point you should have everything cleaned, hung, or folded, and all your out-of-season items out of the way. Now it's time for the famous "use it or lose it" talk that I'm sure you realized was coming. I saved this for after the sorting process so that you could easily see what all you have. (How many black skirts does one person need?) This is undoubtedly the hardest part of working the closet and the downfall of many who try and tackle this task. I'm not going to give you the instructions that always caused me to crumble: "If you haven't worn it in six months, get rid of it." Whenever I heard that advice I would clam up and not take one further step. I'd like to share the guidelines that helped me tackle the closet once and for all.

a. If you have a bunch of clothes from when you were a different size than you are now and you anticipate needing them in the future, fold them all neatly and put them in a container with the size clearly marked on the outside.

b. If you aren't sure whether to keep something or get rid of it, try it on. Go look in a full-length mirror. How do you feel? If you find yourself smiling, promote the article to a hanger. If you find yourself shuddering, give it away — it will look better on somebody else. If you are impartial, grab a container and toss it inside. In six months, repeat the experiment. (Many professional organizers suggest that if you haven't worn something within a year, let it go. I find that often I don't wear something because I have forgotten I own it or I simply can't find it! That's why I suggest the try-it-on experiment.) If you are extremely indecisive, have a friend come over and do a fashion show. I did this once with my best friend. She laughed hysterically at some of the outfits I walked out wearing. We were amazed to find how many items I had kept from eighth-grade. We also discovered clothing that can only be described as "tacky." My nine-year-old daughter (and my sixty-year-old mother, for that matter) would have likely walked on the opposite side of the street if I were to ever wear these items.

c. If you find something that you like but haven't worn for a long while, perhaps you just forgot it was there. I often find a shirt and although I like it, I haven't been "in the mood" to wear it. So before giving it away or tossing it, put it to one end of your closet. This pile will be the "wear it in May (or whatever your next full month is) or give it away" section. Try the neglected item out in your wardrobe. If you like it, keep it, and begin wearing it regularly. If you don't like it (or if you never bother putting it on) then it should be added to the "give away" pile.

d. If you have a hard time letting go of something because it was expensive, a gift, or you have some other attachment, the best cure is to give it a good home. Place it in a bag and deliver this clothing in-person to a homeless shelter or woman's shelter. You'll never regret your decision.

e. If you are weighing whether to keep something or give it away, consider the fabric. One year when I did my spring-cleaning, I was amazed at how many wrinkled clothes were in my closet. I have an anti-ironing gene that I just can't overcome. So here sat all these clothes, never worn, and never ironed. I donated all the clothes and now when I purchase clothes I only buy wrinkle-free items. I have a few favorite fabrics that don't wrinkle and don't pick up pet hair easily. Make sure your fabrics and clothes match your lifestyle.

WHEN YOU SHOP IN THE FUTURE

1. Consider the fabric (see the paragraph above).
2. Try everything on and ask how it makes you feel. Don't add it to your closet unless you absolutely fall in love with it. The last thing you need is another shirt or skirt that you kinda-sorta-like and wear kinda-sorta-sometimes. Even if you find the deal of the century — if you don't fall in love with how the item looks and feels, leave it at the store.
3. Before purchasing clothes, check the care labels. Make sure the care of the item fits into your schedule. I rarely buy items that require hand washing, as I just don't have the time (or desire).

---

4. Tackle socks, hosiery, and intimate apparel next. Throw out anything with a hole or tear. Match up socks. Create a "lost sock box" to keep in the laundry room for socks seeking partners. If you have a dresser with enough drawers, give socks/hosiery a drawer, underwear a drawer, bras a drawer, and pajamas a drawer. If you don't have applicable drawer space, split drawers with a piece of thick cardboard or a wood divider. You can also purchase an inexpensive set of stackable drawers or containers at stores like Office Max or Target. Sort each item into its appropriate category.

5. Tack up nails to hold accessories, purses, and belts. Buy a storage box from your local craft store to securely hold jewelry. (I have a clear plastic organizer that hangs right on my closet rod and has 20 plastic pockets on each side to hold my accessories. I used to have a big jewelry armoire with eight drawers but I found that just took up space! Now with a quick glance I can find what I need via the clear pockets.) Bead and hardware organizers are other good choices for jewelry organizers. Purchase a shoe rack or an over-the-door organizer that easily hangs and holds multiple pairs of shoes.

Your Assignment

Complete steps one through five for a clean and functional closet.

Day 19

Beautifying Your Home

"Learn how to be happy with what you have
while you pursue all that you want."
Jim Rohn

As a frequent traveler, I'm often amazed at how dramatically my mood changes depending on where I am staying. I have stayed in some very nice hotels that were so warm and welcoming I loved being in my room. Other rooms were so dark and uninviting I found my mood spiraling downward. Our environment and surroundings play a huge part in how we feel on a day-to-day basis. Think about it. When your home is messy, chaotic, cluttered, and filled with piles, how do you feel? My guess is "stressed" is amongst the adjectives that top your list. Likewise, when our homes are clean and straightened we feel more at peace.

So why not create a dream home for yourself? You don't need a million dollar budget and a designer's help. Instead, approach your home with the same mentality we bring to this challenge — one day, one step, one project — at a time.

The task of beautifying your home will be an ongoing process. I recommend getting a separate binder for this project. I have a binder with dividers for each room of the house that I wanted to "beautify." Then when I found pictures, ideas, or had inspirations, I would store the information behind the applicable room tab.

The process of going through your home is much like when we created the MASTER TASK LIST. Choose a room in which to start. Sit down for a good twenty minutes, really taking in all the items, furniture, textures, and colors of the room. Then imagine how you would like the room to be. Don't be shy, write down anything that comes to mind no matter how crazy it seems. There may be things on your list that aren't practical right now and that's okay. These notes will give you a clue into the traits and mood you want to create in the room and you may be able to find a less expensive alternative. (For example, in one room I would have loved new hardwood floors. Instead, I found that sanding the current wood floors and covering them with inexpensive rugs purchased at a wholesale outlet, created the nice warm feeling I was looking for.)

Here are some specific things to think about in each room:

COLOR: Do the walls represent the room? If your house has all white walls, consider toying with color. Painting a room is the quickest way to give it a fresh look. Stenciling is another option for those who don't want to brave a full paint makeover. If you want to keep your white walls, are there prints or paintings that could be added to give the room a new tone? What types of prints and paintings would you enjoy — abstract, contemporary, wildlife? What colors should the paintings emphasize to help coordinate the overall color of the room?

FURNITURE: Are there pieces of furniture that need to be refinished, repaired, or replaced? Are there any pieces you would like to add?

WINDOWS: Do you like your current window coverings? If not, what would you prefer? Would you like to go with a valance? Blinds? No coverings?

DECORATIONS: What elements could be added to change the tone of the room? How about a small water fountain in a room where you like to relax? Fountains can be found very inexpensively at stores like Target or Wal-Mart. Would an arrangement of candles or dried flowers add to the room? Could you remove items to simplify the space? Could you swap items with items from another area of the house for a fresh feel?

FOLIAGE: What about plants? Plants quickly provide a new feel within a room. If you have a bad history with plants, don't despair. Visit your local garden center and explain you want a very durable plant for someone without a "green thumb." These garden experts can help you pick the plant that is best for you.

FLOOR COVERING: How do you want your floors to look? Would you like rugs, floor coverings, hardwood, or to lay new tile?

Idea-Gathering

Gathering ideas can be a very fun step. Begin by paging through magazines and finding attractive rooms. For example, if you are working on your living room, begin by finding living rooms that have a theme or feel you would like to emulate in your own home. Don't worry if you can't find something that is exactly like what you want; you can clip furniture from one picture and paintings from another. Here are a few more sources for idea-gathering:

1. If you have a friend who has a "knack" for displays and interior design, consider seeking her help and recommendations.

2. Visit furniture stores, antique shops, and department stores to gather ideas for displays and decoration. Check your local library and bookstore for additional books and ideas.

3. The internet also has a ton of great resources for decorating. Try doing a search at www.google.com for decorating. The Better Homes and Gardens website has a lot of great resources as well — you can find that at www.bhg.com.

4. Visit your local improvement store. Look at their idea books and magazines. Find paint samples and color palettes that are appealing to you.

5. Let the process of gathering ideas take as long as you desire. Remember this is a work in progress. Once you have some ideas, pick one to start. I encourage you to work through one room at a

time, completing it in its entirety before moving to the next room. This way you will be able to enjoy one room while working on the others and not cause a lot of clutter or disruption in the home.

Remember that decorating and performing a facelift to a room needn't be costly or time consuming. Adding a new print to a wall, colorful pillows to a couch, or a few plants can breathe new life into a tired room.

Your Assignment

Begin gathering ideas. Try to choose at least one idea that can be implemented today to beautify your home.

Day 20
Living with Laundry

✵

"People are just about as happy
as they make up their minds to be."
Abraham Lincoln

Did you know that according to the Soap and Detergent Association (SDA), Americans wash more than 35 billion loads of laundry each year? In case you're wondering, that averages out to about 10 loads, per household, per week. No wonder we constantly feel like we are living beneath a pile of never ending laundry — we are!

Getting a system in place for handling laundry can work wonders toward taming this task. Today I'll share with you the system that I use in my own home.

Begin with a well-stocked laundry room: Before we get down to the actual washing and drying, it is important to check your laundry room for supplies. Just like you wouldn't think of having a kitchen without a pot, so should your laundry room be properly stocked. Here are the items I keep in my laundry area:

- A scrub brush (to scrub stains and stain removers into the surface)

- "Solo Sock Box" to store socks without matches, until they find their mate
- Drying rack or towel bar for items that need to air dry
- A "Repair Tub" for anything that needs repair (a button is missing, a tear needs mending, *etc.*)
- A "Dry Cleaning Tub" for anything that needs to be delivered when you run weekly errands
- Iron and ironing board
- Clothes hangers to hang items directly, versus folding only to hang later
- Laundry detergent
- Stain removers
- Fabric softener
- Anti-static Sheets
- An extra tub for hand-washing or soaking

Now it's time to tackle the system for your laundry. Begin by getting a different colored tub for each family member. Encourage family members to use their laundry bins and then take them downstairs when they need washing done. (Hopefully they wash it themselves — but if they don't, then make sure to let them know it is their responsibility to get the bin to the laundry room.) Explain the DRY CLEANING and REPAIR tubs that stay in the laundry room. Let them be responsible for getting their clothes into the right tubs. If you have a designated day for laundry, let family members know when that is and that if they don't have their laundry to the laundry room by then, they will have to-do it themselves or wait for the following week.

Also, make sure kids know *how* to-do the laundry. I remember when my mom taught me how to use the washer and dryer at age eight. She made little labels that made it very easy for me to determine settings. On the washer and dryer she made labels for LEVIS, TOWELS, UNDERWEAR, *etc.*, so I could understand what dial should point where. I thought doing laundry was the coolest thing. I did everyone's laundry for about a year. Make sure to give your kids the chance to take on this responsibility. You may also want to use this as a task in the chore and reward system that we cover on Day 42.

Make a habit of doing a load of laundry each day (if volume warrants). Each morning when I go downstairs, I take a tub of dirty laundry. At night, I carry a tub of clean laundry upstairs.

Your Assignment

Take control of your laundry loads by implementing today's tactics. Get your laundry room stocked with the appropriate supplies and let your family know about any changes in the laundry routine. Begin doing a load of laundry each day, or every other day (depending on volume).

Intermission: Speaking of Laundry Lists... What are You Waiting for?

✵

Take a pen and blank piece of paper and head to your kitchen. Set your stove timer for five minutes. For the next five minutes, write down all the things that you "want to-do." This list should include all those things that "you will do tomorrow," or "start next week," or "when you have some extra time," or "when you have more money," or "when you get that promotion," or "when your children are older," – you get the idea.

After completing this "laundry list" of goals, consider how you would feel if you were able to implement one, two, or more in the weeks and months to come.

Next, look at each goal on this list and try to recall when you initially made this goal. You will probably notice that your laundry list has become longer with time. If you do not take action, it will continue to grow. If it continues to grow, you will continue to be immobilized because there will be too many things on the list.

Instead of letting this list grow, implement at least one goal in the next thirty days. Try to implement another next month. When we choose to make time for these goals, we become invigorated and feel better about our surroundings. As we implement these goals, we also create space for new goals.

Part Three

Information Management

Daily Routine Action List

Days 21 through 37:

- ☐ Complete your gratitude journal each evening.
- ☐ Begin each day with a heartfelt "good morning."
- ☐ Carry your CATCH-ALL notebook with you everywhere.
- ☐ Transfer your to-do list each night.
- ☐ Complete your Nightly Reflection each evening.
- ☐ Each day, use the three-step action list.
- ☐ Consult your MASTER TASK LISTS for any other tasks that need to be completed.
- ☐ Do a daily laundry load if volume warrants.

Day 21
Choosing Your File System

"Minds are like parachutes —
they only function when open."
Thomas Dewar

To begin, you will need the hanging files, manila folders, and file holders that you purchased during the "Setting Up Shop" assignment. Wherever you plan on doing your filing, place your "inbox." I have mine on top of my filing cabinet. This is where I put everything that "needs to be filed." I have tried filing every piece of paper as it comes in but I just wasn't able to stick with it. So I put the paper-collecting box on top and have a "pact" with myself to file all paper within a week.

The key to successful filing is to not make 10,000 categories or files. In our hunt for organization it is easy to make the assumption that the more files we have the more organized we are. Not so. The more files we have, the harder it is to find what we need.

I recommend that everyone begin with some master categories. Depending on where you are in life, your master categories may be different than mine. Before we choose our master categories, let's define what they are. A master category is an overall area of your life. Within the master category, you will have subcategories. Think of the master category as a "view from afar" and the sub-categories are your "zoom" lens. This approach to allows for a more accurate filing system.

Let's look at four options for master categories. Choose the system that feels like a "fit" for your season of life.

By Family Member: Create a master category for each family member. If most of your paperwork revolves around individual family members (health records, school records, *etc.*) this is a good option for you. You can then add one more master category for OTHER things that aren't sorted by family member.

By Task Type: If you work outside the home and bring home a lot of paperwork pertaining to your job, or you have a home-based business, you may want to try FAMILY, WORK, and PERSONAL as your three master categories.

By the CYLC System: I keep my files to match my CATCH-ALL notebook. I have a master category for each of the following: LONG-TERM PROJECTS, SHORT-TERM PROJECTS, LONG-TERM TO-DO ITEMS, SHORT-TERM TO-DO ITEMS, and REFERENCE.

By Letter: If you have tons of files, then try doing everything alphabetically. This is how we file within our company. If you choose to try the alphabetical method, make sure to always alphabetize by the first letter of the actual name. For example, if you have three bank accounts — one held at F&M, another at Bank of America, and the third at M&I, you would file them under "F," "B," and "M" respectively. DO NOT file them all under "B" for bank accounts. Making shortcuts like that will cause you many headaches as your number of files increases.

Lastly, everyone should have an ARCHIVE master category. This is for all the paperwork you need to save somewhere, but won't access very often (old bank statements, tax info, receipts, *etc.*). If you use a two-drawer file cabinet, make one drawer for CURRENT materials and the other for your ARCHIVE and REFERENCE materials.

Think through your paperwork and imagine applying each of the four systems. Which feels the most natural? Or can you think of a system that better matches your style of living? Today, your only assignment is to decide which file system you will use. Tomorrow we will delve into the sub-categories and actually set up the system.

Creating files out of need, instead of creating files just to fill them, is a must for successful filing.

Choosing Your File Home

For those with extremely busy lives and many things to manage, nothing can take the place of a durable filing cabinet. I would recommend a four-drawer cabinet. They can be purchased for between $70 and $100 at most office supply stores.

If your filing needs are not as intense, there are many solutions for holding hanging files. Rubbermaid® makes some large totes that match the size of a regular full-file drawer. There are other totes with handles, crate systems, and more. Take a trip to your office-store retailer and find a system that works for you. You should have a drawer or crate for each master category and then another for your ARCHIVE items. (If you do not have a lot of paperwork, consider using one drawer for two or three master categories.)

Your Assignment

Think through your paperwork and imagine applying each of these systems. Which feels the most natural? Or can you think or a system that better matches your style of living. Today, your only assignment is to decide which file system you will use and make sure you have the supplies required.

Day 22
Subcategories and File Labeling

✵

"Make a game of finding something positive in every situation. Ninety-five percent of your emotions are determined by how you interpret events to yourself."
Brian Tracy

By now you should have all your file equipment and have chosen the master categories you will be using for your files. For each master category you will have a separately labeled file box. Today we will label our files and begin the process of filing a few papers.

To start, put all your papers that need to be filed in a box. You may need one or two boxes for a severe backlog. Later, when your system is current, you will place papers in the inbox you purchased as part of the Setting Up Shop assignment. Look at each paper briefly as you place it in the box. This will refresh your mind on the types of records you need to save and help you choose the best sub-categories for your file system.

Now it is time to pick sub-categories. These will be different depending on which MASTER CATEGORIES you chose. Let's explore options for sub-categories for the four MASTER CATEGORY sets I introduced yesterday.

***NOTE:** Depending on what system you choose, some people find it helpful to color code their files.*

For example, in the FAMILY, WORK, and PERSONAL model, you may choose to make all your WORK folders green, FAMILY folders YELLOW, and PERSONAL folders yet another color. You can also use color-coded labels or a highlighter to achieve the same color-coded results.

EVERYTHING ALPHABETICAL: If you opt for this method, you can probably guess what your sub-categories will be. Each letter of the alphabet will get its own folder. You can write these on blank folders or purchase folders with the letters of the alphabet preprinted on the tabs.

FAMILY MEMBERS: If you use this method, create a master file box with the name of each family member. Your hanging files will include the different categories for each family member like extracurricular activities, medical records, and school (or work) information. Assign each family member an "OTHER" file for any miscellaneous papers. Be careful not to create too many files. Creating too many files is the single biggest reason that systems fail. So start with a few files — then when you notice a family members "other file" getting a bit thick, go through and see what category you could create to thin it out.

MATCH IT UP: If you would like to try my system, then your files will match your CATCH-ALL notebook. Your main categories will be, LONG-TERM PROJECTS, SHORT-TERM PROJECTS, LONG-TERM TO-DO ITEMS, SHORT-TERM TO-DO ITEMS, and

REFERENCE. Within each of these files, create a sub-category for each major item. For LONG-TERM PROJECTS and LONG-TERM TO-DOS, create a file for each and store relevant research, magazine clippings, ideas, or information in the applicable folders. For SHORT-TERM PROJECTS, do the same. I like to put a manila folder in the hanging folder so I can take it out quickly and easily without worrying about those metal tips on the ends of hanging files. On the outside of the manila folder, I like to write the steps needed to complete my projects. For SHORT-TERM TO-DOs you can choose whether each item warrants a folder. If it's something quick and simple that will be crossed off quickly, there is no point in making a file. However, if it's a SHORT-TERM TO-DO that requires a lot of paper (like filling out forms for summer camp) you may choose to give it a file. Sorting items alphabetically within these categories also helps for easy management.

Reusing Files: *Office supply stores sell stickers the size of label flaps. I recommend these so you can simply "label" over used files and they can be recycled many times.*

FAMILY, WORK, and PERSONAL: FAMILY, WORK, and PERSONAL will be your three master categories. Then, as I mentioned previously, use your "to file" box as inspiration for the subcategories you will need. (Consider a three-tier inbox using one tier for work, one for family, and one for personal.) Here are some ideas to get you started: PERSONAL might include all your dreams, projects, goals, recipes, gift ideas, birthday cards, a birthday log, and the like. WORK would obviously include anything that you may need to reference at home that is for work. For FAMILY include major bill categories like utilities, insurance, medical, car payments, loan payments, mortgage or rent, each credit card account, school papers, *etc.* You could also include vacation plans and anything else that applies to family. Don't forget the archive category I mentioned yesterday. This is a must for any effective system.

Your Assignment

Now that you have chosen your system, spend some time today creating the files you will need.

Day 23
Tackling the Paper Pile and Using Five or Ten Minutes Wisely

✵

"People who say it cannot be done
should not interrupt those who are doing it."
Anonymous

I will keep today's reading short to allow you some extra time to tackle your "file pile." Yesterday, you looked through papers and moved them into the to-file box. Today we will tackle an inch or so of the papers that need filing. Make more files, as needed for papers that don't have a home.

The Value of Five to Ten Minutes

I wanted to briefly touch again on the value of five- to ten-minute increments. So many of us have the inclination to wait until we have a "couple free hours" to tackle tough tasks. As you well know, in today's world, "a couple of free hours" do not occur very often! One of the best things I did for myself in terms of time management was to realize how much value rests in five- to ten-minute "lulls" throughout the day. The next time you have five- to ten-minutes between tasks, go ahead and see what you can tackle. I think you'll be amazed (I was) at what a difference this short amount of time can make. Here are some things that I routinely do in my "lulls"...

1. File twenty to one hundred sheets of paper
2. Wipe down all my kitchen counters
3. Light dust a room
4. Sweep the kitchen floor
5. Start or fold a load of laundry
6. On a stressful day, take a five-minute break for positive thought

There are also many opportunities for multi-tasking. You might be on hold on a phone call, during which time you could do some filing or fold some laundry. You might be talking to an in-law that goes on for hours; use this time to complete another task that doesn't require intense concentration. If you are watching television, could you take an inch of your TO FILE pile and the file container and sort through it during commercials?

Your Assignment

Part A: Sort through at least one inch of your "file pile." Schedule a regular time to continue tackling your file pile or use five to ten increments.

Part B: Today, take advantage of all the five- to ten-minute increments that come your way. See what you can accomplish in those "stolen moments." Record your accomplishments in your CATCH-ALL NOTEBOOK.

Day 24
File Maintenance and Bonus Files

"Sometimes we are limited more by attitude than by opportunities."
Anonymous

Today we are going to review some simple filing rules, allowing you more time for catching up on your files and assembling your system.

For starters, I want to mention a few other files that I keep in my system that may be of value to you.

REMINDER: I use this reminder file for anything important that I absolutely have to remember (usually these are deadline-driven). If it's a big project, I still keep it in my other files but I will write the basic premise on an index card or piece of paper and toss it in the reminder file, too. While we still have the CATCH-ALL notebook, this just serves as another "double check" system for me — very important for my busy lifestyle! I try to review this file daily or every-other-day at the very least.

TO RESPOND: If I have incoming mail or email that I need to respond to, but don't have time when I receive it, I print a copy for the TO RESPOND file. I also put phone messages here or bills that need to be clarified or contain inaccurate charges. I take this file with me when I run errands and use my "wait times" to respond to as many things as I can.

TO READ: After throwing away 10,000 pounds of magazines, I have learned not to add to my clutter by keeping every issue that comes my way. Instead, if I get a magazine and don't have time to read it, I rip out the interesting features and toss them in this TO READ file. I also put school papers, catalogs, and anything else I want to glance over inside this folder. This is another great folder to "grab-n-go" when you know you'll have a wait, such as the doctor's office.

BILLS TO PAY: As my bills come in, I put the ones that need to be paid in a file. I review this file twice a month when I sit down to pay bills.

DREAM ON: I added this file to hold all the miscellaneous things that look interesting but I don't have time for at the moment. I hope that I can get to them someday and I certainly don't want to lose them in the interim.

You may not need all of these files. These are just examples that I added to my system out of necessity. I encourage you to adopt those that you feel may be useful to you. Continue to add your own files as you discover your needs for customization.

File Maintenance

In order to keep your file system efficient and useful it's important to-do regular maintenance. Try to make sure you have all your papers in files at the end of each week. Also, choose a quarterly date to purge and "archive" your files. Remove any files that are "completed" or no longer needed and move them to your archive area. Update and add any categories that you may need as you start the new quarter.

The Five Rules of Effective Filing

Let's sum up our file system with the five rues of effective filing. (You may want to print these and post them on the front of your filing system!)

1. **Let your papers dictate the files you create — not the other way around.** In other words, don't make a thousand folders and then find paper to fill them. Instead, start with the basics and add more files as warranted.

2. **Make your system your own.** Explore the different options that I have offered and find the one that works for you, customize it and make it your own.

3. **Make sure that all your papers are filed at the end of each week.**

4. Each quarter, go through all your files and archive what you can. Create and update your system as needed during this quarterly review period.

5. Regularly review your files to keep abreast of all your current activities and events.

Your Assignment

Add any of the "bonus files" that appeal to you. Mark down your file maintenance times in your master task list. Review the Five Rules of Effective Filing.

✎ Post the five rules of effective filing that can be found in the *Companion Workbook* near your file space.

Day 25
Say Goodbye to Junk Mail

✵

"Bless not only the road but the bumps on the road.
They are all part of the higher journey."
Julia Cameron

After all of this filing, you may be amazed at how many papers come into your home. One of the easiest ways to reduce clutter and filing backup is by reducing the amount of paper that comes in your front door. It would seem that the mail contains more paper than we could possible fathom these days — and more temptations to buy, buy, buy!

Today, take a step in minimizing your junk mail by asking to have your name removed from mailing lists. Send a letter requesting that your information be removed from the following lists:

DIRECT MARKETING ASSOCIATION
(simply write your name and address on a postcard)
MAIL PREFERENCE SERVICE
DIRECT MARKETING ASSOCIATION
PO BOX 9008
FARMINGDALE NY 11735-9008

The National Demographics and Lifestyles collects profiles and sells the information. To be removed from their profile system, write to:

NATIONAL DEMOGRAPHICS AND LIFESTYLES
LIST ORDER DEPARTMENT
1621 18th STREET, SUITE 300
DENVER CO 80202

Here are a few more major mail order houses that often rent/sell lists. Odds are you are on one or more. To be removed, submit your request to:

ADVO, INC.
6955 MOWRY AVE
NEWARK CA 94560

DONNELLY MARKETING
DATABASE OPERATIONS
416 SOUTH BELL
AMES IA 50010

METROMAIL
LIST MAINTENANCE
901 WEST BOND
LINCOLN NE 68521

There is also an association devoted to stopping junk mail that will help you to have your name removed from lists. For more information on how to join, write **STOP JUNK MAIL ASSOCIATION,** 3020 BRIDGEWAY, SUITE 150, SAUSALITO CA 95965 or call (800) 827-5549

Your Assignment

Decrease the amount of junk mail coming into your home (while also helping the environment) by requesting your name be removed from these lists. Remember, that each time you request a catalog in the future, you will be added back to these lists unless you specifically request that your information not be shared.

Intermission: Operation Handbag

✵

"Taking joy in life is a woman's best cosmetic."
Rosalind Russell

For many years I carried the world's largest handbag. Weighing in at no less than 25 pounds, I was prepared for every situation. Many shoulder aches later I finally put together a system that allowed me to be prepared for any event while also maintaining a bag that wouldn't break my back. Today, let's give your handbag a makeover to allow you to be prepared for any situation.

First, you'll need to have the right handbag. I have two. The first is a small bag — about 7x6 inches with a long strap so it can easily be slung over my head and under one arm. I like to use this when I travel as it allows me to have both hands free. (It is also more secure than a bag over one shoulder.) I also use this purse when running short errands. My other bag is much bigger — it is a cross between a tote, briefcase, and purse. (Make sure both bags that you choose fit securely over your shoulder so you are not constantly fussing with the strap.) I use this bag when I need to take my camera, or a book, or want to put my CATCH-ALL notebook in the bag. I also use the bigger bag when I am going to dinner with my family and want to take along some crayons or a coloring book to occupy my daughter.

The key to using multiple bags is to make sure that everything can be transferred quickly. Think of setting up your handbag in "stations." Let's look at the different stations you might have in a bag.

The Basics

1. Dollars & I.D.: Obviously, the most common reason to carry a bag is to transport our money and identification. What is interesting is how many extra things we pack into our wallets. Outdated receipts, credit cards, club cards we don't ever use, the family history in photos, and so much more. To avoid packing your wallet, get the smallest, functional wallet that you can find. I recommend just a small wallet that will hold your license, a credit card or two, and your dollar bills. Personally, I rarely use a wallet. When I buy a purse, I make sure it has a small zipper compartment on the inside and just zip my license, credit card, and dollars into that area. As for all my discount and club cards, most places offer one that can be attached to your key chain. I opt for those whenever possible. I keep all my other credit cards and club cards in a business card holder at home. When I run errands, I grab any I need before leaving the house. I recommend staying away from bulky wallets that also hold checkbooks. They are hard to maneuver in a small purse. Instead, keep your change and checkbook separate.

2. Coins: For the past eight years I have used coins as my "secret savings." Whenever I make a purchase, I pay with dollars and never use change. Even if the purchase is $10.02, I will give the cashier $11.00. I just throw my change into the bottom of my purse or bag and then transfer it every other day or so to a large container. That container serves as my "rainy day" money or family vacation money. I am often amazed at how much I can save in so little time. If you choose not to stash your change for a rainy day, I'd recommend a coin purse. The zipper pockets in wallets rarely hold all the change we get in a day or they leave your wallet heavy and lopsided.

3. Checkbook: I keep my checkbook in a basic cover and keep it separate from my wallet. This allows me to optimize storage space in my purse instead of using a bulky wallet. Also, if my husband needs the checkbook, I can give it to him without taking apart my wallet. If I'm running to a place where I only need my checkbook and ID, I can just tuck my license behind my checks and go.

Cosmetics: Have you ever emptied your purse only to find seven lipsticks on the bottom? Or have you needed a powder or other makeup item and it's not there? I keep two or three small cosmetic bags with different looks (*i.e.*, one for nighttime — a bit more dramatic, one for daywear with warm colors, one for daywear with cool colors). In each small cosmetic bag I have the following: mascara, pressed powder, eyeliner, lip liner, lipstick, eye shadow duo, blush, and under eye concealer. I leave these bags by my other cosmetics where I get ready each morning. Then, depending on the day ahead, I grab the applicable bag and add it to my purse, always returning it to my cosmetic area at night.

To Do Stations: If you are heading to a doctor's appointment or another location where you will likely have some extra time, take your bigger bag and add something from your to-do pile. I like to keep some blank note cards in a plastic bag. When I go somewhere I can add this to my purse and catch up on writing notes and cards to friends. The TO READ file or TO RESPOND file from your file system are other good choices.

Other items for your handbag:

- If you are a contact lens wearer, I would recommend including a small bottle of solution and an extra pair of contact lens, and an extra case (good to keep in a plastic bag in case of leakage)
- Sunglasses
- Hairbrush or comb
- One or two wet naps
- Your actual or a photocopy of your health insurance card and auto insurance card
- Emergency contact information (and who to notify in case of an accident) tuck this in your wallet or next to your ID.
- Small note pad
- If you take medications, a 24-hour supply of your medicines in case you are unexpectedly stranded somewhere
- Pen
- Needle and thread (the small travel sewing kits you get at hotels work perfectly)
- Band-Aid® or two
- Envelope: If you travel a lot or need to keep receipts, buy a poly-envelope to store them in for safekeeping

For any of the above items you choose to take with you, package them in a small bag within your purse.

Your goal is to not have any loose items roaming around. Instead, you'll have a combination of small bags that can be easily transferred from one carrier to another. You also won't have to spend an hour digging when the woman behind you in the "speedy-checkout" line is sighing condescendingly.

Your Assignment

Grab your handbag and dump out all the contents. Using the tips above, develop bags and small "stations" to store all of your items.

Part Four

✵

Recreating the Family Dinner

Daily Routine Action List

Days 21 through 37:

☐ Complete your gratitude journal each evening.
☐ Begin each day with a heartfelt "good morning."
☐ Carry your CATCH-ALL notebook with you everywhere.
☐ Transfer your to-do list each night.
☐ Complete your Nightly Reflection each evening.
☐ Each day, use the three-step action list.
☐ Consult your MASTER TASK LISTS for any other tasks that need to be completed.
☐ Do a daily laundry load if volume warrants.

Day 26
Mastering Meal Planning

✵

"Consider the postage stamp; its usefulness consists in the ability to stick to one thing until it gets there."
Josh Billings

Meal planning seems to be one of the most commonly-battled tasks among home managers. A recent study showed that at 4 PM, seventy percent of people have no clue what they are having for dinner — and eighty percent of families only have dinner together once a week. Looking at those statistics, its no wonder that fast-food and unhealthy-convenience foods are a billion-dollar industry and we are facing unprecedented weight gain in our children. In addition to the nutritional decline, these facts show how our families are losing the magical moments brought only by meal times. In one of my first books, *Back to Basics: 101 Ideas for Strengthening Our Children and Our Families*, I had an entry called RECREATING THE FAMILY DINNER. I compared how our great grandparents had meals together two to three times *per day* while we are lucky to have one meal together two to three times *per week*. The family meal acts as a "mini family meeting" where we come together and share our days and our lives. When we lose that, we begin to lose touch with one another.

I bring these statistics to your attention because I feel they offer inspiration and further commitment toward the MASTERING

MEAL PLANNING section of this challenge. My goal is to help you create a plan to have a homemade meal together at least five nights per week. By the time we finish this section, you will have a weekly plan of family-approved recipes, complete with shopping lists. Before we get started, let me just run through a few frequently asked questions.

What if we are all running every which way during the dinner hour? Set a time by choosing when the MOST family members can be present. Stick to this time every day. Let everyone know that THIS is when dinner is. As they make future arrangements, let them know that you expect them to work around the dinner hour. If they don't, that's okay. Don't cancel the dinner hour because someone can't attend. You owe it to yourself and other family members to prepare a healthy, quality meal — and more importantly, to sit down on a regular basis and enjoy a mealtime.

There is only me (or myself and one other person). Should I cook a full meal every night? My husband travels three to five days per week and we usually don't know until 24 hours beforehand when he will be gone. This makes meal planning very difficult. In the past, I often had dinner planned and then if he would leave I would just feed my daughter and not worry about my meal (or just make a snack). But then I realized that my daughter deserved the sit-down dinner hour. Now we have dinner together regularly — no matter what.

Those are the two things I hear more frequently when I talk to home managers about meal planning. There are other common questions pertaining to the meal-planning process but those will be covered as we work through it. Soon you will have your own two to four master meal plans. Each one will have a week's worth of meals with all the recipes and shopping list attached. Basically — you will never wonder "What's for Dinner?" again. Let's get started.

YOU WILL NEED:
Four file folders
Index cards or paper

Begin by gathering all your recipes into one place. This includes those you have clipped out and were "going to try" and also any tried-and-true recipes. When I did this, I also gathered my cookbooks. I am a cookbook-a-holic. What amazed me was out of the 10,000 recipes contained within a given cookbook, my family would only eat three. Instead of having this huge tome that I would never page through, I just ripped out the recipes I was interested in trying and gave the cookbook to another cookbook-lover. This really made all my recipes assessable. If you choose to-do this, don't try to get through all your cookbooks in one day. Break this down. This is an easy task to-do while watching television or watching a child at a sporting event. To make the project portable, just place sticky notes as bookmarks on the pages you will keep, and then tear them out when you get home. If ripping out a page makes you cringe, copy them onto another piece of paper and leave the cookbook in tact. Or, for the time being, place each recipe you like on an index card. For example, if you had a book called *100000000 QUICK AND CALORIE-LESS RECIPES*, and you want to try the BASIL CHICKEN, on the index card you would write the book title, the recipe name, and the page number.

Please label your folders as follows:

- **EVERYONE LIKES:** These are recipes you have tried which all family members enjoyed.
- **ADULTS LIKE — KIDS DON'T:** With taste buds varying so dramatically by age, you may have quite a few recipes that Mom and Dad like, but leave the kids less than thrilled. Place those in this folder.
- **KIDS LIKE — ADULTS DON'T:** Likewise, you may have 10,800 pasta recipes for kids — yet the adults in the household are on a protein diet. Place the recipes that are popular with kids but uninspiring to adults, in this folder.
- **WOULD LIKE TO TRY:** If you come across a cool recipe that sounds good but you haven't made it yet, place it in this folder.

For today, your assignment is to go through and place each recipe into one of these files. Again, if you are a cookbook-a-holic like I am, don't worry about doing all of these today — just do a chunk. We just need to have enough to put together our first weekly menu plan.

Your Assignment

Create your four file folders. Begin sorting recipes into the applicable folders.

Day 27
Streamlining Your Kitchen

"If at first you don't succeed,
you're running about average."
M.H. Alderson

The kitchen is the "central hub" of most homes. For this reason, we will be devoting quite a few days to making this hub welcoming and efficient. You'll notice that several of the daily challenges in this section may seem "insignificant" compared to other items we have tackled. However, it is often the "little things" that become big stressors in our lives. I have identified some of the most common stressors, and now we will work to eliminate those from our lives.

We will keep today's assignment short, sweet, and simple so you can keep sorting those recipes! By the way, stop and give yourself a pat on the back if you have made it thus far. Did you know that most people don't make it past day 14 of a new project they start? You are in the minority. You are committed and will make this happen.

Grab a cardboard box or two, make a cup of green tea, and head to the kitchen. Open your first food cabinet or pantry. Grab any box that has been there for more than three months. Examine it with the following criteria.

CHECK THE DATE: Does it expire? If it does and it has, throw it out. If it's going to expire soon, put it on a special shelf in the cupboard reserved for items to be used quickly. If it doesn't expire, but has been there for more than two months, ask yourself what you are planning on doing with it. If the answer is anything other than "eating it soon" put it in a cardboard box to be taken to your local food bank. (If you do not have a local food bank, check with local churches. Many have regular food drives. Schools also have frequent food drives.)

Move through each cabinet like you did the first. Then:

STORE LIKE ITEMS TOGETHER: Once you have streamlined, it is time to sort. Place your canned items together — grouping by veggie, fruit, soups, *etc.* Place your snacks together, cereals together, *etc.* This goes with one of the first organizing principles we learned: "KEEP LIKE ITEMS TOGETHER."

CONSOLIDATE: While you're at it, make sure to consolidate containers. If you have three bags of open pasta, combine them into a large plastic container or bag.

SIMPLIFY SETS: How many cups, coffee mugs, and dishes do you have? If you have too many, stow some or give some away. One day my husband pointed out that I had collected thirty-some coffee mugs, however I was the only one who drank coffee. I chose a few that I liked to replace cardboard pen/pencil holders and then donated the rest to our local charity. Make sure you don't take up prime kitchen space with rarely used items. Likewise, if you have special china or holiday dishes, stow those away until needed.

MIX AND MATCH YOUR TUPPERWARE®: Find all your Tupperware®, Rubbermaid®, and other containers and match the tops to the bottoms. I'm always amazed at how I end up with 10,000 bottoms and only four tops. Match every top to its bottom and then throw out the tops and bottoms without homes, or use the bottoms to hold cosmetic items, office, or craft supplies.

Your Assignment:

Streamline, store, and consolidate. When you finish, you might still have a few minutes to sort recipes before tomorrow's assignment.

***SIDE NOTE:** When I did my own streamlining, I actually had four boxes of Pasta-Roni® that had moved from Milwaukee to Portland — lived in the cupboard there for five years, moved back to Milwaukee and lived in an apartment cupboard for eighteen months and then moved into my new home and new cupboard! What exactly I planned on doing them with — I'm not sure! I think I bought them because they were a "good deal" but never got to cooking them. Now I have a policy to never keep any food that is older than my daughter.*

Day 28
Making the Meal Plan

✵

"Life itself is the proper binge."
Julia Child

For today's assignment, you will need your recipe folders. We are going to begin sorting these into "Weekly Menus." Think about next week. What recipes would you like to eat? Look through the recipes that are "FAMILY APPROVED" and pick the majority from there. Now add a recipe from the folder containing just RECIPES THAT ADULTS LIKE and remember to choose one from those that JUST THE KIDS LIKE for that evening.

As you choose meals for your meal plans, consider the following:

1. Do you usually eat out in a given week? If so, you may want to plan for five or six days instead of a full seven. I always do my plans based on five days. I like doing it this way because I don't end up with spoiled food or leftovers that are not used.

2. Try using the same "main ingredient" to minimize costs and spoilage. For example, you might want to feature beef one week and chicken another.

Don't use any recipes from your WOULD LIKE TO TRY folder when you create your MASTER MEAL PLANS. Since you are going to put some work into making the shopping lists for these, you want them to be permanent. It wouldn't be fun to have to remove one recipe because it wasn't a hit and then find all of its ingredients on the shopping list. I like to-do my regular meal plans and then on weekends experiment with new recipes. These come from the WOULD LIKE TO TRY recipes. From these recipes, I add the ones that get the "thumbs up" to FAMILY APPROVED file.

Once you have a group of five to seven recipes, place them in your CYLC Binder behind the RECIPES tab. I like to put mine in plastic sheet protectors. That way, when I cook I can pull out the page I'm working with and easily wipe off splatters.

You should also decide how many WEEKLY MENUS you would like to have ultimately. This can be determined by how often your family will eat the same food. If they don't mind eating the same thing once each month, then ultimately you will want to create four weekly plans. (You don't need to create them all now; add one or two when you are feeling creative. Be flexible to adding more since you are bound to find more recipes that you would like to add from the WOULD LIKE TO TRY file.)

The initial menu setup will take some time. It's well worth it though because in the future you won't have to worry about what's for dinner or if you have the needed ingredients on hand. If you aren't into making your own menus there are books that feature weekly meal plans. I created a book with nineteen weekly meal plans that we use in our home titled, *The Rush Hour Cook's Weekly Wonders* (ISBN 1-891400-14-2). The book contains nineteen weekly meal plans complete with shopping lists and then many bonus chapters like smoothies, healthy recipes, instant-family dinners (just add families), desserts, and more. To learn more or to order an autographed copy visit www.rushhourcook.com. I also have a free email based newsletter called THE DAILY RUSH. Every Monday through Friday it delivers a recipe to your email box along with a tip, piece of trivia, or idea for the day.

Your Assignment

Choose the recipes you would like to use for your first weekly meal plan.

✎ See the master shopping lists and sample menus provided in the *Companion Workbook.*

Day 29
Create Your Master Shopping List

❋

"If you chase two rabbits, both will escape."
Anonymous

Now that you have at least a week's worth of meals gathered and pasted into your CYLC Binder, we are ready to create your MASTER SHOPPING LIST. I make mine in pencil first. Once perfected, I type the list into the computer and print extra copies. At the top of the page I list the recipes in the meal plan, then all the ingredients follow. Then when I decide to make that "week of menus" I can just grab a blank list, check off the items I already have, and run to the store to grab the remaining items. As I said earlier, the time investment for this part of the system is a bit tedious, but once you have your weekly menus in place you'll be glad for the nudge in this direction.

Begin by looking at a recipe and writing down the ingredients by group — *i.e.*, produce, canned goods, pantry/spice, meat, dairy. Move onto the next recipe and add its ingredients to your list. If it uses the same ingredient as one of the previous recipes, increase the amount already on your list. For example, if you have a recipe that calls for two onions and then come across a recipe that needs another onion, change your "two onions" to "three onions." (You can see why pencil works well the first time around.)

Once you have finished listing out all the ingredients, you are almost done. Check to make sure you have enough side dishes to serve with your main entrees. If you don't, add bread, salads, pasta, and other side dishes to your shopping list. I have uploaded a sample weekly meal plan that you are welcome to use at www.rushhourcook.com/menusample.pdf

Your Assignment

Finish off your first weekly menu plan using the previously recommended steps. Shop for your first Weekly Meal Plan so you can try it during the next full week.

Day 30
Analyzing Your Kitchen Functionality

✵

"If anything is worth trying at all,
it's worth trying at least ten times."
Art Linkletter

While we are in the kitchen, let's take a quick glance at how our kitchen is set up. Are we maximizing the space and its functionality?

KITCHEN CHAOS: When people come in the door they naturally place everything they are holding in the first convenient space they come across and this is often the kitchen counter or dining room table. Having a designated drawer for each family member in either of these rooms can help nip this in the bud. If you don't have drawer space, purchase a plastic stackable drawer unit from Walmart, Target, or Office Max. Label each drawer with a family member's name. There is one exception to this rule — you should definitely have an extra drawer or space in the kitchen. Since the kitchen is often the "heart" of the home and like it or not we spend a lot of time there — cooking, unpacking groceries, retrieving drinks, and doing dishes, most of the time you will be in the kitchen when someone will ask something of you, or try to pass off some homework to sign, or a bill to pay. Having a drawer where you can safely store these action items makes them easier to find later.

You may also want to hang a set of hooks or put a coat rack right by the door to easily collect backpacks and coats, which might otherwise end up on the kitchen counter or a dining room chair. etc. (Don't ask me why, but it seems hooks are so much more successful than hall closets with hangers.)

KITCHEN FUNCTIONALITY AND SET-UP: Take a moment to look at your kitchen as a professional designer would. How is it set up? Does it maximize space and exemplify functionality? Here are some questions to help determine the level of functionality in your kitchen. Make changes where necessary. If you don't have enough time to make all the changes today, add them to your short or long-term to-do lists.

RELEVANT PLACEMENT: Are dishes, pots, pans, *etc.*, near the item where they will be used? For example, is bakeware near the stove? Are mugs near the coffee maker? Are your microwaveable dishes near the microwave? Are glasses near the refrigerator? Are spices near the stove? Are non-food items (batteries, plastic storage containers, etc.) stored in non-prime space? If you answered "no" to most of these — consider a complete kitchen overhaul and empty all of your cupboards. Then place items in functional locations. Warning: this can take a whole day since you will want to wipe down the cupboards while they are empty. Make sure you save it for a day when you are up to conquering the kitchen. Better yet, if you are doing this program with a partner, work on your kitchen one weekend and hers another. This will definitely make the process more fun and you are more likely to see it through to completion.

COUNTER SPACE: Is your counter space kept as clear as possible or do you suffer from the knick-knack bug? If your counter is covered with trinkets, mementos, canisters, and the like, think of another place for these items. Keep your counters clear for maximum ease in the kitchen. You can also take "regular counter items" like knife storage blocks and mount them beneath cupboards to free up additional space. Or add hooks for pans and cutting boards to create more room.

KITCHEN CLEANER: Remember when we set up our cleaning caddy for each bathroom? Do the same for your kitchen and store beneath the sink. (If you have children either store these cleaning caddies higher or install childproof locks.) Keep bleach wipes, glass cleaner, oven cleaner, towels, and the like in your caddy. Each night after dinner, pull out the caddy and do a quick scrubdown. (This is great to assign as a chore, too! We will be covering chore and reward systems shortly.)

A GOOD WIPE DOWN: While you're analyzing the above items, go ahead and give your kitchen a good "wipe" down. Wipe down your counters, your cupboards, and other surfaces. To save yourself some scrubbing, go ahead and spray all your appliances and counters before you start "analyzing." Let your cleaners sit while you complete the other parts of today's assignment. Wipe down when done. For any caked on food or stains, boil some water on your stove and carefully pour a small amount onto the area. Let sit for a few minutes and then wipe away.

GOOD KITCHEN PRACTICES: Get in the habit of emptying your dishwasher each morning. This way it is free to collect dishes during the day. After dinner, dishes can go straight into the dishwasher instead of piling up on your counters and waiting for a turn to be cleaned. At night, make a habit of running your dishwasher. This way you can start each day fresh.

Taming the Refrigerator and Freezer

Take a garbage bag (or two or three) as you head to the kitchen. To begin, we are going to clear out the refrigerator. If you have multiple refrigerators/freezers, or they are packed beyond belief break this down into manageable steps and add it to your MASTER TASK LIST. Today, focus on getting the "door" of one refrigerator done, tomorrow tackle the drawers — then a couple of shelves, etc.

Beginning with the door, take out each item. Check the expiration date and throw away anything that is expired or you don't plan on consuming by its end-of-use date. Place everything else on your counter.

As you run across plastic containers or nearly empty items, (a gallon tub with one tablespoon of butter inside) consolidate into a smaller container.

You'll need another caddy for corralling condiments. I have found it to be a great timesaver to store all breakfast condiments and lunch/dinner condiments in a caddy. This would include salad dressings, catsup, mustard, jellies, extra McDonalds® sauces, etc. This prevents these little items from taking up big space and makes them easy to find. (It also makes setting the table a snap.)

Once you have all the items out of the door, move onto the drawers and shelves continuing to thin and consolidate as opportunity allows. When an area is empty, spray it with cleaner. Let the cleaner sit while you tackle another spot. Then wipe down.

It shouldn't take long to whip through your refrigerator and thin and consolidate the innards. When you have completed that task and wiped down the shelves, take a look at all the items you have. Place like items together, back in the fridge, being careful to maximize space by placing your most-accessed item near the front.

KEEP IT UP: I try not to wipe down my refrigerator too often as my goal is to be organized and efficient — not a cleaning maniac. Here is how I keep things simple: When I get groceries each week I make sure to clean out any leftovers and do all my consolidating. Then I wipe down at least two shelves. The next week I wipe down a different area. By rotating what I wipe down, I only have to-do a "full clean" once or twice a year.

Your Assignment

Complete the "kitchen analysis" above to assess your kitchen's functionality. Make changes where necessary. Put together your "cleaning caddy" and wipe down kitchen surfaces and appliances. Clean and consolidate your refrigerator and freezer using today's guidelines. If you have a major refrigerator and freezer task ahead of you, break it down into manageable segments and add it to your MASTER TASK LIST.

Intermission: Beautiful

✵

"I live by a man's code, designed to fit a man's world, yet at the same time I never forget that a woman's first job is to choose the right shade of lipstick."
Carole Lombard

If you are among the ten percent of women that are not serial-cosmetic purchasers, you can skip this Intermission. However, if you own more than ten lipsticks, this day is for you. (Or if you own more than three eye-shadow compacts and one has blue eyeshadow or is ten years old or older.) Many women are drawn to cosmetics like a magnet. Before we know it, we are buried in every possible color, brand, shade, and option. Good makeup and skincare can make us feel wonderful. The wrong makeup and skin care can have the exact opposite effect.

Today we are going to trim our "make up stock" to a few simple looks that are quick and complimentary. Everything else will be given away, pitched, or stored.

As a fellow makeup-a-holic, I can honestly say I have tried just about every brand. I have bought-in to the "lose your crow's feet in three days" and other promises of expensive skin care. I have now trimmed back my makeup and skincare routine to my "tried and true" products. They are effective, complimentary, and yield a simple routine. I will share my "favorite" products with you today, but before we do that, let's trim back your own "stock."

1. **Sit down near your makeup with a mirror and a mug of coffee or tea.**
2. **Start with lipsticks and a good bottle of makeup remover.** Try each one on. If it is dry, throw it out. If it is more than a year old, throw it out. If it makes you look like a clown, throw it out.
3. **Move on to foundations and powders.** If they do not blend into your skin seamlessly, throw them out. If they are cakey, throw them out. If they are more than one-year old, throw them out.
4. **Repeat the above with blush and eyeshadow**, throwing out any colors that make you look or feel clown-like.
5. **Analyze all your skin care products.** If it doesn't work, throw it out. If it is more than one-year old throw it out. Repeat with mascara, eye-liner, and any other products.

(Important note: if you can't bring yourself to throw out these often-expensive items, at least put them in a bag so we can get them out of the way for now.)

If you have been following the instructions, you have likely trimmed down your collection immensely. Go ahead and clean your face so you have a "fresh palette." Using the colors you have left, experiment until you find a look "you love." For some this may be just a foundation, blush, and lip gloss For others it might include three or four more products. Once you find a look you like, store the items in a small cosmetic bag or plastic bag. Create another look if you like and put it in a second bag.

The goal is to have everything that makes us feel good (and that hasn't expired) easily assessable.

✎ The *Companion Workbook* contains a five-minute makeup routine and a list of my personal favorite tried-and-true products.

Part Five

✵

Relationships, Romance, and Friendships

Daily Routine Action List

Days 21 through 36:

- ☐ Complete your gratitude journal each evening.
- ☐ Begin each day with a heartfelt "good morning."
- ☐ Carry your CATCH-ALL notebook with you everywhere.
- ☐ Transfer your to-do list each night.
- ☐ Complete your Nightly Reflection each evening.
- ☐ Each day, use the three-step action list.
- ☐ Consult your MASTER TASK LISTS for any other tasks that need to be completed.
- ☐ Do a daily laundry load if volume warrants.

Days 36 and 37:

- ☐ Complete your gratitude journal each evening.
- ☐ Begin each day with a heartfelt "good morning."
- ☐ Carry your CATCH-ALL notebook with you everywhere.
- ☐ Transfer your to-do list each night.
- ☐ Complete your Nightly Reflection each evening.
- ☐ Each day, use the three-step action list.
- ☐ Consult your MASTER TASK LISTS for any other tasks that need to be completed.
- ☐ Do a daily laundry load if volume warrants.
- ☐ Host a daily "Happy Half-Hour."

Days 38 and 39:

- ☐ Complete your gratitude journal each evening.
- ☐ Begin each day with a heartfelt "good morning."
- ☐ Carry your CATCH-ALL notebook with you everywhere.
- ☐ Transfer your to-do list each night.
- ☐ Complete your Nightly Reflection each evening.
- ☐ Each day, use the three-step action list.

- ☐ Consult your MASTER TASK LISTS for any other tasks that need to be completed.
- ☐ Do a daily laundry load if volume warrants.
- ☐ Host a daily "Happy Half-Hour."
- ☐ Practice the Five-Minute Relationship Miracle daily.

Day Forty:

- ☐ Complete your gratitude journal each evening.
- ☐ Begin each day with a heartfelt "good morning."
- ☐ Carry your CATCH-ALL notebook with you everywhere.
- ☐ Transfer your to-do list each night.
- ☐ Complete your Nightly Reflection each evening.
- ☐ Each day, use the three-step action list.
- ☐ Consult your MASTER TASK LISTS for any other tasks that need to be completed.
- ☐ Do a daily laundry load if volume warrants.
- ☐ Host a daily "Happy Half-Hour."
- ☐ Practice the Five-Minute Relationship Miracle daily.
- ☐ Review your value card daily.

Day 31
Organizing the People in Your Life

✵

"I used to think that being nice to people and feeling
nice was loving people. Now I know it isn't.
Love is the most immense unselfishness
and it is so big I've never touched it."
Florence Allshorn

In this phase of the challenge we will be exploring the relationships that you maintain (or feel obligated to maintain) in your life. Many management systems overlook this crucial point. I find this interesting since who we spend our time with accounts for the majority of our life. We are social beings, not hermits. Even if we want to be a hermit, daily demands make it impossible. Our time with one another is the key component to our quality of life. However, if we don't "organize and choose" who we spend our time with (and how we spend that time) we can find ourselves feeling discontentment, anxiety, or depression.

Today we will take the first step in selectively choosing who we spend our time with and how we spend that time.

STEP ONE: Grab Your Calendar

Before we can go any further, we need to find ALL the people we are spending time with at least monthly. Your calendar will be of great help. As you make this list, do not include appointments (like dentist, hair, *etc.*), which are "musts" in life-maintenance. Include the people that you CHOOSE to see (going to lunch, coffee, stopping by someone's house) and those you feel OBLIGATED to see (your husband's-cousin's-sister's-brother). If you work outside the home, also include co-workers that you go to lunch with or do "extra" activities with. And of course, you'll need to include your family members. You will find the worksheets for this section in the Appendix. Begin with the worksheet titled "Organizing Our Relationships" and record the names in the left-hand column.

STEP TWO: How Much Time Do You Spend?

Next to each person, write down how much time you spend together (on average) each week. If it is someone you see only every other week, or monthly, write that down too (once a month for 60 minutes). Don't worry about being exact — approximations will work just fine.

Your Assignment

Record the names of those people you spend time with on the left-hand side of the Organizing the People in Our Life List worksheet (see the Appendix).

 The *Companion Workbook* contains copies of each worksheet needed for this phase of the challenge.

Day 32
How Are You Affected by the People in Your Life?

✵

"The kindest thing you can do for the people you care about is to become a happy, joyous person."
Brian Tracy

Yesterday we made a list of the people who we are either obligated or choose to spend time with. Today, we are going to "rate" how that time affects our lives. Have you ever hung around someone who had absolutely NOTHING positive to say about anything? After an hour of listening to her, how did you feel? What about spending time with someone who is just brimming with life and happiness? How did you feel after an hour of time with her?

Whether we like it or not, we are greatly influenced by those we spend time with and that influence can be positive or negative. It is true that we do have control over HOW WE REACT to things — however, who wants to spend all their time trying to react positively to negative people? We can't always be doing "cognitive reprogramming." It's much better to make wise choices and spend our time with the people that compliment us. That's doesn't mean that everyone has to be "high on life" but it means that we limit those people who are likely to bring us down. By spending most of our time with positive people, we reserve some energy to positively influence the negative people that we do choose (or have) to be around.

Let's examine how each person on the list you made yesterday influences you. Please read through the categories that follow and assign each person from your list to a category. This will go right next to their name in the PERSONALITY RATING column of yesterday's worksheet.

NOTE: If someone ranks in more than one category, you can list both categories under their personality column rating. And yes, family members fall into these categories too!

1. **Perfectly Pleasant Patty**: These are the people whom you love to spend time with. The time is healthy, upbeat, inspiring. You wish you could spend more time together. You leave your meetings feeling good about yourself, the world, and very invigorated.

2. **20/80 Katy**: These are people whom, for the most part, you enjoy. They are fun, encouraging and appreciate you for who you are and encourage you in what you are trying to achieve — most of the time. There is an occasional bump in the road, a bit of negativity here and there, and perhaps a tad of gossip, but no one is perfect!

3. **50-50 is Kind of Nifty Nelly**: These people are caught between the glass being half-empty and half-full. They tend to be positive

half of the time, but counteract that positive-ness with negativity the other half of the time.

4 Sinking Sally: Sinking Sally is on a ship that is slowly sinking due to negative thinking and choosing immobility over action. Although she would like to think she is on the path to change, she is a lot of "talk" and very little "walk." This type of person often seeks your advice (often over and over again about the same problem) but never takes positive action. She is more interested in pondering change than creating a positive life.

5. Gossip Gloria: Gloria won't be changing her life any time soon. In fact, why should she, since she lives vicariously through everyone around her and has plenty of ideas on how to change their lives? (She'll share those ideas with you, whether you want to hear them or not.) Can you say, Gossip Gloria = bad news?

6. Surface Sarah: Sarah seems positive on the surface; she may even be an outstanding citizen or churchgoer. But when you get to know Surface Sarah, you will find that although she talks a good talk, she often has bitterness, jealousy, or rude things to say about others. Surface Sarah can seem so wonderful and generous on the outside it can be hard to realize what lurks beneath that shiny surface.

7. Controlling Carla: Carla knows exactly how you should live your life and she is going to tell you. She is possessive, controlling, and downright bossy.

Your Assignment

Add the "type" of person each person on your list falls into, choosing from the seven categories described. (Add additional categories if needed.)

Day 33
Making Positive Changes with People

✵

"Keep away from people who try to belittle your ambitions. Small people always do that, but the really great make you feel that you, too, can become great."
Mark Twain

You should now have a list of the people you spend time with monthly and an assessment of how that time affects you. Now let's take a good hard look at what needs to be changed and make some plans for changing it.

1. Do you have at least one Perfectly Pleasant Patty?
IF YES: Do you see this person at least once a week (or talk with them on the phone)? If yes, GOOD — keep it up. We all need a Perfectly Pleasant Patty to help lift our spirits, inspire us, and engage us, at least weekly. If the person you have on your list does not have that much time (you won't know until you ask — and even a five minute call will do sometimes) then you need to go hunt down another Perfectly Pleasant Patty. I encourage you to spend at least sixty minutes each week with this type of personality (more if you can).

IF NO: Then it is time to be on the lookout for one. Perhaps you could even find one through the Change Your Life Challenge Partner Match. Since we are all engaged in this challenge, because we are looking for positive change, my guess is that there are quite a few inspirational and fun women reading this book. Spending time emailing or talking on the phone is just as effective as spending time together in person. I encourage you to spend at least sixty minutes each week with this type of personality (more if you can).

In the CHANGE TO BE MADE column, write down what you need to-do here. Do you need to keep doing what you're doing? Find another (or a first) Perfectly Pleasant Patty? Write down your task and of course, make a deadline, and schedule it in your calendar.

2. How many 20/80-Katys do you have? These are the most common long-lasting friendships. They weather the ups and downs of life and remain mostly encouraging and positive. Sometimes when we get busy with life, we forget to really keep in touch with the 20/80-Katys. Days go by and before we know it, it has been weeks or even months since we have spoken. The 20/80-Katys are very valuable foundations for our lives. Have you been spending time each week or every other week with your foundation-friends? If not, how can you change that? Record it in the CHANGE TO BE MADE column (and of course, write down on your calendar when you plan to implement that change).

3. How many 50-50 Kind of Nifty-Nellies do you have in your life? Think of these people as "break-evens." They might enrich your life some, but for the ways they enrich it, they also counter-balance with negativity. To be quite blunt here, these people simply take up your one non-renewable resource — time. They do not move you forward, but at least they don't drag you backward. You should certainly try to spend less time with these people and more time with the "Katys" and "Pattys." How could you do that? Record your thoughts in the CHANGE TO BE MADE COLUMN.

4. Are you trying to save a Sinking Sally? As women, we often feel the need to nurture and rescue. I have tried to save many-a-Sinking-Sally. On the upside, it often worked. On the downside, it can be quite overwhelming. Of course, we make the world a better place when we take someone who wants to change (but may need an extra push here and there) and help them. I believe that is important. However, I have learned the hard way that we can't try to save a bunch of people at once, or we will deplete our own energy and end up becoming a Sinking Sally ourselves. Try to limit the Sinking Sally's in your life to one at a time. If you need to make any changes in this category, record it in the CHANGE TO BE MADE column.

5. Cutting Loose the Controlling Carlas and Gossip Glorias: You can probably guess what I am going to say here: WHY ARE YOU SPENDING TIME WITH THEM? There is no benefit for your life here. These people sap your joy and your energy. Write three simple words in The CHANGE TO BE MADE column: Cut them loose.

6. Have you uncovered a Surface Sarah? It can take a while to see the "other side" of a Surface Sarah. In fact, you may have become so close by the time you see the other side that you find it hard to believe that "could really be her." Surface Sarah's are master manipulators. Learn to exit out of awkward conversations quickly. If after a month you don't see improvements, say so long to Surface Sarah's.

You likely have noticed that I am more adamant about how to handle certain personality types than in other areas of the challenge. This is because I know for a fact that hanging out with the wrong people (or talking to them for that matter) is the single-most influential outside force in my life. The Surface Sarahs, Gossip Glorias, and Controlling Carlas DO NOT WANT TO CHANGE but they do WANT TO CHANGE YOU — and it's not for the better! This doesn't mean you need to ex-communicate them completely, but you do need to severely limit your exposure if you truly want to lead a healthy life.

Handling Obligations

Now, some of these people you may be OBLIGATED to see. For example, your in-laws may be Sinking Sallys but if you plan on making your marriage work, you must adapt and live with it. However, before you commit to spending time together, make sure it is a true obligation. Sometimes we think we "should" or "ought" to-do something — when in reality that expectation is from an outdated belief system. If it is a true obligation, ask yourself: Can it be minimized? For example, if you see your in-laws every other week for a three-hour dinner, could you change that to a once-a-month dinner? Or could you change the dinners from three hours to two? Doing so may not be easy, and you may catch "a bit of flack," but that is short-term. You will be creating a long-term change that is much more healthy for you — and thus much more healthy for your immediate family.

Your Assignment

Analyze your findings and record the changes that need to be made in the CHANGE TO BE MADE column. If you are spending most of your time with unhealthy or toxic people, look at how you can free up that time for the people that bring positive energy and inspiration to your life.

Day 34
Connecting

✵

"The walls we build around us
to keep out the sadness also keep out the joy."
Jim Rohn

Your assignment today has two parts — one that can be done via phone and one that can be done via mail. You will be using the "Prioritizing Our Relationships" worksheet to complete today's assignment. (This worksheet can be found in the Appendix and in the *Companion Workbook*.)

There are three columns on this sheet:

A. People I need to communicate with more (whether that be email, phone, or in-person)

B. People that are just fine and should remain status quo

C. People I need to spend less time with

Transfer each name from the Organizing Our Relationships worksheet to one of these columns based on your findings yesterday.

Next, grab the phone. Skim down the first column, where you have listed those people you need to communicate with more. Call one and let her know you are thinking about her. Call another person from this list (or ask the first person you called) if she can get together within the next thirty days. Set a date. Voila — part one done. (Don't let me stop you though — keep on moving down the list if you're game. Keep in mind that the more time you spend with the people in column A the more joy and contentment you will find.)

Part two of your assignment today is a fun-filled field trip. Grab your checkbook, grab your list, and head to the card store. Purchase a collection of cards to keep near your CYLC Headquarters. There is nothing like a hand-written note, especially in today's world where most everything is done via email. Take your time and make an afternoon of it. Browsing card shops can be so much fun. If you like, take your address book along and find a nice coffee shop. Sit outside (unless its winter or rain) and enjoy an afternoon of writing cards. Send as many notes as you can to the people in Column A (send at least two). You have now completed part two of your assignment.

(Note: If you are the creative type, consider visiting a crafting superstore, rubber stamp store, or scrap-booking store instead of a card store. Buy supplies to make your own cards. There is nothing like the homemade touch. If you don't have time to make a lot of homemade cards, intersperse them with store-made cards.)

Lastly, go back to the Organizing Our Relationships worksheet and under CARD/COMMUNICATION write down the date that you connected. This will help you remember whom you still need to connect with and also help monitor how much time goes by between communications.

Bonus Ideas

MAKING LETTER WRITING EASY AS 1, 2, 3: Want a simple way to keep in touch and brighten other people's spirits and in turn brighten your own? Carve out an hour each week as "card time." Sit down and go through your cards and choose a few to send. To make this simple, I strongly recommend you print labels for frequently used names/address. If you have MICROSOFT WORD this is very easy. You can quickly make a sheet of labels to keep handy. Just go to the HELP area and type in MAKE LABELS and easy-to-follow instructions will appear.

I print a full sheet of labels for each person I communicate with regularly. (There are thirty labels on a sheet.) Then keep a variety of envelope sizes handy. When you come across a cute comic, neat article, child's artwork, photograph, or other tidbit you would like to share, (1) toss it in the envelope; (2) add a label; (3) mail. It's as easy as 1, 2, 3!

A MINI-MAILING STATION FOR KIDS: You can help your kids keep in touch with relatives by adapting the same strategy. Make labels for relatives and provide a drawer for envelopes, labels, and stamps. Encourage kids to send drawings and notes. You may even want to make a "CARD HOUR" for kids.

If you are drowning in kids' artwork and don't want to throw it away, pass it on. A picture from Junior would likely brighten another relative's day.

Your Assignment

Make contact with someone you need to spend more time with and arrange a "date." Then take your address book and have a field trip to a card store.

Day 35
Here's Looking at You

"Our outward life is a mirror
of what we feel and believe inside."
Brook Noel

The past few days we have been analyzing people in our lives and how they affect how we feel. Just as important is how we affect others. Today, I would like you to assess yourself.

Review the personality type descriptions we worked with when Organizing Our Relationships. Imagine a friend listing you on their worksheet. How would you be classified? How would you like to be classified? One of the interesting things to note is "like attracts like." If you gossip a lot, you're likely going to find a plethora of Gossip Gloria's at your beck and call. If you are a 20/80 Katy, don't be surprised if your list has mostly these personality types. Remember, our lives are reflections of what we are inside.

Write down how you would classify yourself (whether you like it or not). ______________________________

Write down how you would LIKE to be classified.

____

These answers will be important as we move into the self-nurturing part of the program. Also, just by becoming aware of your response, you may find you make different decisions because you realize where you are, and where you would like to go. Whenever we turn off "auto-pilot" and substitute awareness, we start the engine of change.

Your Assignment

Consider what personality group you fall into and what personality group you would like to be in. What steps can you take toward change if there is a discrepancy between the two?

Day 36

Who Is That Person Across the Table?

"Be kind and merciful.
Let no one ever come to you
without coming away better and happier."
Mother Theresa

Today we will begin focusing on our relationships within the home. We will look at how we interact with our kids and our significant other. If you are child-less or significant other-less, don't think you get the day off! There are still plenty of important relationships that you can improve with these tactics.

A while back, I was reading an article in a women's magazine that compared the life of a married woman with children, to the life of a single woman without kids. In the article, the married woman said something to the affect that once you have children there is little time for your spouse. You just hope that when the kids are grown and gone, you married someone that you will still want to spend time with.

The statement struck me as sad but true. When my marriage hit its own tumbles, I felt the same way. I remember sitting at the dinner table watching my husband eat and thinking: *Who is that person?* While I thought I knew him, it suddenly occurred to me how far apart we'd drifted with the demands of work and family. Our lives were changing and evolving rapidly, yet we hadn't kept each other informed on many of the changes or shared in the growth. Instead, we took for granted that we knew each other, when in reality, we were drifting apart.

As soon as we realized this was occurring, we set out to change it. My husband and I carved out our own ways to stay connected and stay close. Here are some ideas that worked for us and may work for you.

TAKE WORK HOME: One of the rules we've heard is that you should leave work at the door and not take it home. Yet, if many parents are working forty to sixty hours per week, work becomes half of our waking hours. By not sharing this time, we cut out a huge piece of our experience. Your partner should know what is going on at work, who you like, whom you don't, *etc.* Sharing this part of yourself will help your partner understand your joys and frustrations.

MAKE A DATE: No matter what it takes, go on a date at least every other week. It doesn't matter if you go out for breakfast, lunch, dinner, or a walk — just make sure that every other week you *connect* without children.

EXPRESS YOUR NEEDS: Teamwork is the glue of a successful marriage. When we can anticipate our partner's needs and offer our help, we make the days easier. Let your partner know how he can help you and find out how you can help him. Never assume that "he should know" how to help you. Express your needs clearly. Likewise, don't assume that you understand his needs, ask.

CREATE GOALS TOGETHER: Share your dreams and ambitions. Create common goals that you can work toward together.

Your Assignment

Stop for a moment and put down this book. Call and find a sitter or relative to watch your children and make a date with your partner. Write it down on the calendar and plan a fun time together. Try to-do this every two weeks and take turns planning the date.

IF YOU'RE SINGLE: Don't think you are off the hook for today's assignment. You need to make sure that you are spending quality time with other people as well. So take today to book a "date" with a friend.

Day 37

Host a "Happy Half-Hour"

✵

"Life is what we make it.
Always has been, always will be."
Grandma Moses

Adults have long reaped the gratification that "Happy Hour" can bring. It's that great hour when the "work" is over and we can relax, sit back, and enjoy focused time with friends.

Today parents spend an average of seventeen to fifty minutes of quality time with their children. Partners spend even less quality time together. Given these statistics, we would do well to adopt a universal "Family Half-Hour."

When kids and parents get home from school and work, have some appetizers on the table. This doesn't need to be creative—peanuts (shell'em for more fun) and popcorn are perfect choices. Add some bottles of root beer or fancy glasses filled with juice or sparkling water. Sit back, relax, and enjoy one another.

If you do not have children, spend this time with your partner. If you do not have a partner, invite someone over to connect with or meet someone on a regular basis for enriched quality social time.

Your Assignment

Tonight, surprise your family with a "happy hour." Keep conversations light, upbeat and encouraging.

Day 38
Treating Each Other Well

"Your children will see what you're all about
by what you live rather than what you say."
Wayne Dyer

Relationships are vital to our emotional well-being. The examples we set in our own lives send a strong message to others. When you look at your own marriage or relationship, remember that you are sending messages to your child about how a relationship should be. Is your relationship a good model for future relationships your child might have?

While meeting the demands of day-to-day life, it's easy to let the "little things" that make a difference slip away. Be conscious of how important the "little things" are in a relationship. Be grateful for each other and remember to express this gratitude. There is a quote about how when we look back in reflection, we often discover "little things" make up a "big thing." Below are some ideas for keeping a relationship strong and setting a positive example through "little things."

SHOW AFFECTION: Affection, touch, and words of support have proven to be of significant importance to both our physical and emotional well-being. Display emotion and support regularly in your household.

WORK OUT DISAGREEMENTS: When conflicts arise, talk them through. Don't walk away or leave an issue unresolved since this will send out the message that conflict should be avoided rather than resolved.

COOPERATE: Work together to meet the day-to-day challenges of maintaining a home, meeting the demands of work, and rearing children.

MAKE TIME FOR EACH OTHER: Remember that before there were children, there was your relationship. Nurture this relationship and allow it to grow.

TAKE A STROLL DOWN MEMORY LANE: While working toward the future, remember to relish the past. Recall favorite times together, journeys you have taken, and stories that you love.

HOLD HANDS

DWELL ON THE POSITIVE: Instead of focusing on the qualities your partner doesn't have or the things he doesn't do, focus on the positives. Think for a moment about all the great qualities that your partner has and what drew you to him in the first place. Focus on the positive to perpetuate growth and appreciation.

THANK YOUR PARTNER REGULARLY: Taking one another for granted is one of the most frequently heard complaints from married couples. Remember to thank your partner.

MAKE DAILY TIME TO CONNECT: Even if it is just five minutes, a daily time to touch base, compare notes, and share ideas is vital to a healthy relationship. With our hectic schedules, if we don't make time to connect, we are bound to find ourselves feeling disconnected from our partner.

Your Assignment

Today, thank your partner for something he or she has done for you. Connect for at least five minutes.

Day 39
The Five-Minute Relationship Miracle

"They may forget what you said,
but they will never forget how you made them feel."
Carl W. Buechner

The Five-Minute Miracle works in any type of relationship — relatives, spouse, children, colleagues, friends — you name it. The premise is simple. Here's how it works:

1. Choose a relationship that you ***know*** needs some work.
2. For five minutes ... give that person your total attention. What does that mean?

a. **Listen only to them**: ignore your own thoughts, don't worry about your response, just listen
b. **See them as they are**: don't project traits or qualities onto them, simply see them as they are right then
c. **Make eye contact**: use touch where appropriate, communicate with your body language remembering that ninety percent of communication is non-verbal.

Each and every day, use the five-minute miracle within one of your relationships. You may find it hard to be that focused (it's not easy) which is why we only do it for five minutes. I guarantee though that by doing this focused exercise you will learn A LOT about communication that will affect you outside of your designated "Five-Minute Miracle " times.

Your Assignment

Choose someone whom you want to improve your communications with and practice the Five-Minute Miracle.

Day 40
Defining Your Values

✵

"Our value is the sum of our values."
Joe Batten

Recent years have brought a lot of conversation about family values. While values are now openly discussed in society, many people still don't clearly know their own value system.

Several years ago I gave a keynote speech at a conference for mental health professionals in Washington State. I asked each attendee to take a piece of paper and a pencil and write down their three core values — within thirty seconds. Out of the three-hundred attendees, only a handful of professionals could complete the assignment. In my work, I have become convinced that not living by our priorities leads to our imbalance, which leads to our depression, which leads to poor health. Aligning our lives to our values is the first step we must take in order to create a healthy life. The second step is actually living by the values we identify.

Professional speaker Glen Van Ekeren offers the following powerful ideas and questions for helping to define values:

"Defining your values is not just an academic exercise. Rather, it is a down-to-earth step toward realizing fulfillment in life. Carl Rogers said, 'Clarifying your values is the first step toward a richer, fuller, more productive life.' To clarify your values, ask yourself: What do I believe in? In what guiding principles can I become constructively obsessed? What governs my life? What do I stand for? What puts meaning into my life? What qualities are important for my life to be complete?

"This is not a simple exercise. Grasping for the right words is normal. Values are not contrived on the spur of the moment, given to vacillating, or negotiable principles that come and go with each passing day. Rather, they are ingrained in the fiber of a person's heart and soul."

Your Assignment

Realize that before you can find true contentment, you must know your core values and then align your life by them. Use today's questions to explore your values and when you discover your core values, write them on an index card to review daily. Use these core values as a light to guide your life.

✎ Additional exercises for exploring values can be found in the *Companion Workbook*.

Part Six

✵

Super-Mom

Days 41 through 45:

- ☐ Complete your gratitude journal each evening.
- ☐ Begin each day with a heartfelt "good morning."
- ☐ Carry your CATCH-ALL notebook with you everywhere.
- ☐ Transfer your to-do list each night.
- ☐ Complete your Nightly Reflection each evening.
- ☐ Each day, use the three-step action list.
- ☐ Consult your MASTER TASK LISTS for any other tasks that need to be completed.
- ☐ Do a daily laundry load if volume warrants.
- ☐ Host a daily "Happy Half-Hour."
- ☐ Practice the Five-Minute Relationship Miracle daily.
- ☐ Review your "value-card" daily.
- ☐ Give your children a self-esteem booster each day.

Day 41
Self-Esteem Boosters

✵

"We worry about what a child will be tomorrow, yet we forget that he is someone today."
Stacia Tauscher

Children with healthy self-esteems try harder in school, get along well with others, hold a "can-do" attitude about life, and feel positive about their environment. They can accept ups and downs graciously. The opposite is true of children who suffer from low self-esteem. These children compare themselves to others and never feel they have done well enough. They are frustrated easily and fear risk and challenge. Children with a low self-esteem can easily fall prey to peer pressure, eating disorders, and other dangers.

By using a positive, can-do attitude in your home, you will pass that attitude on to your child. Try the following ideas to encourage a positive self-esteem.

Examine yourself and your attitude: Children learn by example. If you hold a high self-esteem and think positively, odds are your child will, too. If you suffer from a low self-esteem, you will need to examine your current patterns of thinking and work on changing them.

Seek out the positive: This does not mean you need to be a Pollyanna, but you should search for the positive side of things. When your child comes to you with a problem, ask questions and pursue the positive side. The same goes for how you act in your own endeavors. When things go wrong, look for the upside.

Why ask why? If your child uses statements like "I can't" or other statements that show he is frustrated or giving up, ask "Why can't you?" Asking these questions may frustrate your child and you may hear answers like "I don't know ... I just can't!" Return to the topic later, when the intensity of the situation has lessened. Then ask, "Earlier today you said you could not solve that puzzle. Why don't you think you could solve it?" By exploring reasons together you may find the source of a low self-esteem.

Identify strengths: Another way to increase self-esteem is to emphasize a child's strong points. If he is good in art but doesn't do well in sports, work with him and praise him on his art. By developing a feeling of confidence in one area, that confidence may spread into other areas of a child's life.

Use praise and encouragement: Praise and encouragement are essential vitamins for a child. Encourage all children and praise them for situations where they put their "all" into it, no matter what the result. Filling your vocabulary with positive statements and providing a positive environment is a big step in helping your child build a healthy self-esteem.

Your Assignment

Think of self-esteem boosters like daily vitamins. Offer at least one to your child each day.

Day 42
Giving Up the Cape

❋

"I find it interesting that the very cape I tried to use to fly, became so heavy it kept me grounded."
Brook Noel

One day I was racing around town, errand to errand, mission to mission. When I stopped at my house to grab a few papers, the phone rang. It was a dear friend, so I carved out ten minutes to tell him about the hectic pace I had been leading for the past twenty-four hours.

The night before there had been a full-Wisconsin blizzard and I had gone out to shake the snow off my old rosebush so the branches wouldn't crack under the weight. While doing this, I heard a crackling sound. Looking up, I saw several sparks shooting out from a neighbor's tree. A wire, weighted down with snow, was blowing against a fork in the old oak. Realizing this was probably a fire hazard I called the fire department. The fire department asked me to call the electric company. I did. The woman on the other end said there were emergencies left and right due to the storm.

"But what about my flaming tree?" I asked.

"Well, we can't get to it until we fix the power outages. Would you mind just keeping an eye on it?"

"I guess not," I replied before hanging up the phone.

So I made a makeshift bed near the window using a few sofa pillows and set up my "tree stakeout." While I'm watching this thirty-foot tree crackle and spark, I realize if the tree were to crash down, it would go through our roof. Realizing this could be a disaster, I rushed upstairs to rescue my husband and daughter who were both sleeping soundly.

I shoved him, pushed him, and finally awoke him from his slumber to tell him the tale of the sparking-tree. My husband stared at me through his one half-opened eye. It's obvious he doesn't want to move downstairs and is more concerned with his sleep than his safety. Fortunately, after a little prodding, I persuaded him to join me in my tree-stakeout. I then rescued Samantha from her crib; she was about eight-months old at the time.

We took our perch and Andy made a longer makeshift bed for him to sleep on. Determined not to lose sight of the tree, I tried to stay awake. Despite my best citizen-watch attempt, I fell asleep. Samantha did too, tucked securely between my husband and me.

I awoke around two that morning. I glanced out the window. The tree was still there. Andy was still there. Samantha, however, was not. I shook Andy's shoulder. "Where's Sammy?"

"I'm not sure," he replied, shaking himself awake.

So we began our search. Samantha had just begun the rolling phase and had rolled through three rooms and was on her way, full speed, to the kitchen. Nestling her in my arms, I resumed my place in our living-room-camp.

Samantha woke up two very short hours later with a scream like that of an elephant seal. Knowing this was probably one of her chronic ear infections, I bounced into action with my cooing and cuddling routine. I began to count the hours until the clinic would open. There were four hours between the clinic, and an antibiotic, and me.

After a sleepless, scream-filled, four hours had passed, and a quick shoveling of the snow to get the car out, I ran Samantha to the clinic. There, my suspicion of an ear infection was confirmed. Then it was off to the pharmacy. Then it was back to the house. That morning a call had come from the forestry service. They would be coming out to take a look at the tree and wanted to make sure I was home.

Then it was off to my computer desk where I balanced Samantha on one leg while finishing an advertising campaign with my one free hand. Of course, the campaign was due at the photographer's that day. To deliver the campaign, I would have to drive 45 miles in a blizzard with a sick child, around the schedule of the forestry service.

In my rush to meet deadline, I forgot the ad as I hurried out of the house. So I had to-double back. As I pulled it off my desk, the phone rang. It was a dear friend asking how my day had gone. I informed him of my adventures with the tree, the forestry service, the clinic, and the campaign.

"It's always something," he said in a soft voice. Though I couldn't see him, I knew he was smiling.

"What do you mean?" I had asked.

"Last week when I called it was training your cat, starting a new book, and accepting a new campaign. The week before that it was making homemade edible clay with Sammy, giving painting lessons, and starting a novel while re-wallpapering the kitchen. Why are you doing so much?"

"Well," I paused. "I...um..."

"Yes?"

"I don't do that much," I said meekly.

"You're going to go with that?" he questioned again. I remained silent. Then my dear friend said four words that were a gift: "Give up the cape."

Shortly after that day, I began to-do just that. Instead of trying to accomplish everything and please everyone, I began to focus on what was important to me and my family. I began to accept that there will never be enough time to-do everything so we must do what is important. We must decide and take action on what matters.

Since I've discarded that cape, I've been much less restricted. I find it interesting that the very cape I tried to use to fly, became so heavy it kept me grounded. Instead of living up to the "shoulds" and "woulds" that bound my life, I live by the desire to create harmony within my family. It's a great cape to outgrow.

Participating in soccer, cleaning, cooking, sewing, working, party-organizing, PTA, and church choir doesn't make a person better than one who might only do three activities. Society has taught us that the more you have and the more you do, the more successful and fulfilled you will become. The odds are, in fact, that the person engaged in frequent activities is more likely to become haggard, frustrated, or burnt-out.

I think this is definitely an area where turning back to basics would do us good. Today, when making any decision, contemplate the thought that "less is more."

Your Assignment

In what ways have you been trying to-do more than is realistically possible while still staying sane? Begin shedding the super-parent cape by stripping back unrealistic expectations. Try listing out all your responsibilities and expectations. Then imagine this list was not your own, but that of a dear friend. What advice would you give her for leading a more balanced life?

Day 43
Tackling the Kids' Rooms

✵

"Sometimes it is easier to just close the door."
My Mom

Childless or are your kids grown and gone? Then take this time to catch up on your other assignments, or apply these principles to another busy room in your home — like a study, den, or craft room.

In an ideal world your kids will help you conquer their room, but life doesn't always work that way. I have found that tackling a child's room becomes easier when they are not around. If my nine-year-old daughter is around, a productive cleaning time turns into a long discussion about what we would keep and what would go (including gum wrappers) or we would get sidetracked by a card game or karaoke machine.

If your children are older, privacy will be an issue and you shouldn't go in and tackle the room. In this case, I strongly advise that unless things are growing in there — just leave it alone. That is the route my mother took as I was growing up. She will tell stories of the horrendous mess in my room. Keeping it clean became a constant battle. My aunt assured her that, "A messy room is a sign of intelligence, creativity and busyness." (Thanks Aunt Jo!)

She decided that it was better not to fight and nag over my room and instead she opted to close the door. Consider the importance of your child's room in your overall scope of household duties. Is this an area where you could minimize your involvement? If so, skip the rest of today. If not, read on.

My daughter is still at the age where she loves it when Mom cleans her room. However, don't think you are sentencing yourself to eternal cleaning duty. You are going to-do the "major pass" but then your child will be in charge of maintenance. You'll "step in" twice a year to help trim and refine, but for the rest of the time your child is in the driver's seat. I encourage my daughter, Samantha to-do a "Ten Minute Clean Up" each night as part of her bedtime routine. We return toys from downstairs back upstairs and quickly put them away. We often do this together to make it more fun for us both.

As you work through your children's rooms, you will use the same bins and basic guidelines that we used in the second phase of the challenge. As you use these bins, you will undoubtedly come across some items that might be hard to identify. Pick up these miscellaneous pieces and parts and put them in a box. You have a couple of options for these pieces and parts:

Throw them away: I get so tired of picking up the same pieces and parts, season after season, I usually choose this option.

Use them in arts and crafts: Puzzle pieces can be glued to picture frames or used for other crafts. Go ahead and get creative!

Let your child create new games with the pieces: Although this guarantees the pieces will stay around a bit longer, it does provide creative entertainment.

Tactical Considerations

If you visit an elementary classroom, you will notice that the rooms are often set up in stations. This is a good practice to adapt for younger children. In my daughter's room, I created a "book nook" with inexpensive shelving. I created a "doll area" with some plastic blinds. I used a cubby to corral her arts and crafts, and then placed this cubby beneath a folding table. While a child may have difficulty keeping an entire room clean, she can often keep at least a station or two neat and tidy.

Stations also help children focus on a given task as they are not sidetracked by non-related items.

Your Assignment

Decide what involvement you want to have in the maintenance of your children's rooms. Use the six bins and today's tactics to begin taking control of these rooms.

✎ *Companion Workbook bonus:* A step-by-step guide to hosting sanity-saving family meetings can be found in the workbook.

Day 44
Using Chore and Reward Systems with Kids

❋

"Man is always more than he can know of himself; consequently, his accomplishments, time and again, will come as a surprise to him."
Golo Mann

Childless, or are your kids grown and gone? Then take this time to catch up on your other assignments. For the rest of you, here is the chore and reward system that I have used with my daughter successfully for many years. Try something like this with your own children. The system combines a visual reminder and positive reinforcement and has worked wonders for me, and many others.

Chore and reward systems are incredibly effective and beneficial to children. A good system can inspire children while teaching them responsibility and discipline. It also allows you to delegate some tasks to children and remove them from your personal to-do list. I have found these systems are more effective than allowances, since they visually show children how to choose a goal and work toward it.

The basics: A chore and reward system is a visual tool that lets children perform household tasks in order to earn something they would really like.

Make a list of what you need help with: If you had it your way, what would you delegate around the house? Perhaps cooking, or cleaning-up after dinner? Does laundry or dusting make you cringe? What about taking out garbage or mowing the lawn? Write down any responsibilities you'd like to delegate that are *age-appropriate* for each child.

Next, ask your children to tell you something they would really, really like: Find a picture of this item and place it on a piece of construction paper. Using your list of tasks, create a "road" that leads to the item. As they complete each task, initial it, and once they work through the road they get the requested item.

Chore and reward systems can work with children as young as two! True they won't be very efficient at vacuuming but there are ways they can help make the days go smoother. Building self-esteem at age two and teaching responsibility are also incredible gifts for any child.

I used this system when my daughter was only eighteen-months-old. Using a piece of construction paper I made twenty 1x1 inch squares. At the bottom I made one large square and put a picture of an Elmo helium balloon. Each time she cleaned up her toys, was a good listener for the day, got dressed without a fight, went to sleep without a fight, or went to the bathroom "on the potty," I let her choose a sticker to place on a square. (The stickers were all her favorite characters and animals, dinosaurs, Barney, butterflies, *etc.*)

When the sheet was full, we made a special adventure out of purchasing her balloon. We went to the store and bought only the balloon, taking great care to pick one out. Sammy took the chart with us and proudly explained it (as best she could) to the cashier.

Your Assignment

Choose an end-goal with each of your children for their chore and reward system. Create their charts so you will be ready to begin using them during your next full week. Use your MASTER TASK LIST to help generate "steps' that can be used in the reward system. If you assign a task as part of the reward system, write the child's name in the DELEGATED column of your MASTER TASK LIST.

✎ A copy of my hand-drawn goal chart for my daughter is included in the *Companion Workbook.*

Intermission: Wood Chips, an essay

I wanted to share with you one of the most valuable lessons my daughter taught me when she was sixteen-months-old. I call this essay, "Cherish Your Wood Chips."

Today was one of those days where I just couldn't get enough done. No matter how many times my pen scratched off a to-do list item — a new one seemed to appear. But you, Samantha, didn't have anything on your agenda.

At sixteen-months your days are usually quite free. I sat in my home office, routinely punching computer keys, and you came to my office gate. You had your coat, draped over your head, looking like a little green goblin.

"Samantha we can't go outside today. For one, it's cold and secondly I just have too much on my plate." One of your blue eyes peered out questioningly from beneath the green cape. You then walked to the door and pounded on it. I realized that working was futile — you wanted to go play.

I glanced at my watch, if we hurried we could be back in thirty-minutes, enough time to satiate your needs for the outside world without interfering with my needs on the inside world.

Together, hand in hand, we walked down to the park. I was ready to take you on your favorite swing. Instead, you plopped down in a pile of wood chips. I watched half in amazement and half in frustration as you scrutinized each one. Turning it. Tasting it. Feeling it.

I let out a sigh and situated myself on a low monkey bar. *I don't have time for this*, I thought. I didn't say the words — but Samantha, I had brought you here to swing. I had brought you here to play. And since you were just examining wood chips — I thought of the ways this time could be better spent. My to-do-list ran through my mind: change the laundry, answer e-mail, finish pre-pub issue, respond to Eric's galleys, finish Ken's marketing campaign, send kit to Scholastic.

I let out another sigh and was about to pick you up and take you home, when a little boy approached. I watched as you excitedly ran to him. You displayed each proud find — each beautiful wood chip.

The little boy smiled like it was a holiday as he accepted each offering. When your hands were empty, you ran back for more.

The boy continued to smile. He was with his grandmother — and while she paused for your sixty-second exchange, she then hustled him along saying, "We need to get on the swing so I can get back and finish dinner."

You watched the boy on the swing. It was like a silent communication. You knew, he too, would rather be playing with the wood chips.

After about ten minutes on the swing and a few glances at her watch, the grandmother caught the young boy and began the descent home. Your gaze followed him — and Samantha, you don't have a poker face — you were sad. You plopped back into the wood chips and began to pick them up again. One by one. You had no dinner to fix. You weren't even hungry. The only thing of importance were the wood chips and someone else who could understand their magnificence.

I was saddened a bit as I watched you there. Eventually you will have dinner to cook, you might have your own kids to take to the park, laundry to-do, or a boss to reckon with. Somewhere, somehow, you will learn the constraints of our world. But not today.

As I watched you, I realized I could be like the grandmother and pull you from the magic land of wood chips and take you back to the world of time and accountability. But in that instant, I knew I needed those wood chips too.

So I went down next to you. I on my back, in light colored clothes — immersed in a pile of wet, muddy wood chips; you in your jeans, kneeling, intently handing me each one.

We made the chips into a necklace. We built them into a tower. We stuck them down our shirts. We played catch with them. We pretended they were pizza. We imagined what they would say if they could speak. We smiled at them and pretended that they smiled back.

People mulled around the park, taking their dogs for ten-minute walks, skipping along on their thirty-minute jogs. I am sure they thought we were crazy.

When I next glanced at my watch, two hours had passed. We both had wood chips in our hair and mud on our clothes, but I don't think either of us has ever looked more beautiful.

You stood up, ready now, to go home. And I took your hand and we walked together.

When we got home — I took out a pen and paper and in big black lettering I wrote: "Cherish Your Wood Chips." I stuck it in my daily-planner, right across from my to-do list.

Samantha, when I woke up this morning, I didn't know you would hand me one of the secrets to happiness. When I awoke this morning, I did not understand the value of a wood chip.

Part Seven

✵

Living a Simpler Life

Day 45:

- ☐ Complete your gratitude journal each evening.
- ☐ Begin each day with a heartfelt "good morning."
- ☐ Carry your CATCH-ALL notebook with you everywhere.
- ☐ Transfer your to-do list each night.
- ☐ Complete your Nightly Reflection each evening.
- ☐ Each day, use the three-step action list.
- ☐ Consult your MASTER TASK LISTS for any other tasks that need to be completed.
- ☐ Do a daily laundry load if volume warrants.
- ☐ Host a daily "Happy Half-Hour."
- ☐ Practice the Five-Minute Relationship Miracle daily.
- ☐ Review your "value-card" daily.
- ☐ Give your children a self-esteem booster each day.

Days 46 and 47:

- ☐ Complete your gratitude journal each evening.
- ☐ Begin each day with a heartfelt "good morning."
- ☐ Carry your CATCH-ALL notebook with you everywhere.
- ☐ Transfer your to-do list each night.
- ☐ Complete your Nightly Reflection each evening.
- ☐ Each day, use the three-step action list.
- ☐ Consult your MASTER TASK LISTS for any other tasks that need to be completed.
- ☐ Do a daily laundry load if volume warrants.
- ☐ Host a daily "Happy Half-Hour."
- ☐ Practice the Five-Minute Relationship Miracle daily.
- ☐ Review your "value-card" daily.
- ☐ Give your children a self-esteem booster each day.
- ☐ Follow your morning routine.

Day 45
A Crash Course in Simplification

❋

"Slumps are like a soft bed.
They're easy to get into and hard to get out of."
Johnny Bench

We are almost done with the backlog and basics of housekeeping. This would be a good time to check in on your MASTER TASK LIST and see how well you have done in following it to date. If you are finding it hard to keep up, take the least important task and complete it less often. Continue to shift tasks in this manner until you can keep your head above water without feeling overwhelmed.

Today we will be focusing on organizing strategies that you may implement in any room of your home. You can apply these strategies to your dining room, living room, or any other room that still needs some work. We will also review some simplifying strategies — many of which we have covered, but are always good to review.

KIDS STUFF: In looking around my living room, I am always amazed at how quickly kids' items migrate. It seems that I just helped put away a load of toys when magically another appears. After many a night of "group clean up" I decided to change my system. I purchased a three-drawer cart for my daughter. It is quite small and on wheels. The top shelf has crayons, pencils, books, and the like. The other two shelves are for her toys. When she wants to play in the living room she simply rolls her cart to her play destination. When she is done playing she is expected to return all the items to her cart and roll it back to the closet area. I know other parents who have done this with crates and tubs. I like the cart because you don't have to dump everything out to get to a single item and she can push this cart back and forth versus needing me to lug a heavy crate around.

CHECK LOCATIONS: Are your items located conveniently to where they are used? For example, if you frequently play games in the living room, are they stored in a nearby closet making them easy to retrieve and put away? Try to keep items near the area where they are most often used.

MAGAZINE BASKET: Don't let magazines take over all the surfaces of your rooms. Put a nice basket in one or two rooms and store all magazines within.

REMOTE BASKET: Use a small basket to corral all your remotes into one spot. Put some batteries in the bottom of the basket so you have them when needed. If you find a remote that works more than one piece of electronic equipment, store the others in a safe place (not in the basket). Place your television view guide in the basket or beneath it.

Ideas for Simplification

Read through the list below and highlight any sentences that "speak" to you as positive reminders of how to simplify your life.

- "Use it or lose it" is the golden rule of simplifying one's life.
- If you can't figure out how or what a gizmo or gadget does, then all it's doing is taking up space.
- Take ten minutes every night to unclutter. Have a race with your kids to put everything away. If you do this nightly as part of your bedtime routine you avoid the danger of letting your house get out of control.
- Tackle one project at a time. Whether the project be cleaning, organizing, reading a book, or working on a craft project. Finish each project completely before purchasing or starting another.
- Storage solutions should be kid-friendly. Use carts when you can. Hang hooks that children can reach. Hang closet rods low enough that they can put away their own clothing and coats.
- Limit junk drawers to one in your entire home.
- Teach "the art of simplicity" to your kids.
- If you don't have a place to put something don't buy it.
- Avoid making space for more clutter.

- Don't keep catalogs. They are not only clutter-building, they are a temptation to spend money.
- Donate your books to the local library when you are finished with them. (Ask for a receipt, as the donation may be tax-deductible.)
- Don't become obsessed with saving everything for a later use. How many plastic and paper bags does one person need?
- When you are organizing and come across something you kind of like but don't really use, try to think of someone who not only likes it but will also use it. Make their day by giving it to them.
- Every couple of months tackle the sock drawer. If there isn't a match now, there probably won't be one later. Toss solo socks, or make sock puppets with your kids for some inexpensive family entertainment.
- Don't waste time looking for warranties, manuals, or important receipts. Create a special drawer where only these things are kept. Using a drawer eliminates the chance of the papers never making it to a file or being misfiled.
- Try the following for a quick way to manage your incoming mail and bills. Purchase three magnetic envelope-size holders. Place these on the side of your refrigerator. Use the top one for bills you need to pay with your first paycheck each month. Use the second for the bills that come out of your second paycheck. The third is for all outgoing mail and a roll of stamps. When you receive your mail

each day sort it right by the bill-holders. Throw out envelopes, special offers, and all the clutter that comes with bills these days. When it comes time to pay your bills, remove the top holder and find a quiet place to-do your paperwork. Then return that holder to the middle and move your second paycheck holder up to the "next paycheck" position.

Your Assignment

Highlight those ideas that are valuable to you and begin implementing them. (Make sure to choose at least one.) Review your MASTER TASK LIST and make any needed adjustments.

Day 46
The Morning Crunch

"Gather the crumbs of happiness
and they will make you a loaf of contentment."
Anonymous

Do your mornings feel more like a push and pull contest rather than a smooth preparation for the day ahead? Finding items that need to be taken to school, feeding pets, walking dogs, last-minute planning on who will be home when, getting everyone dressed, coping with the child who'd rather be sleeping, and making breakfast, are just a few of the commonly reported challenges that parents conquer every morning. There are tips and tricks to alleviate the morning crunch. Try the following for a smoother morning routine.

The thirty-minute prep: If morning feels more like a race track than a time of controlled preparation, practice the 30-minute prep. Ease morning responsibilities by preparing all you can the night before. Have children set their clothes out, put toys away, and pack their school bags before bed. Set your own clothes out. After dinner routinely set the breakfast table complete with cereal boxes, bowls, and silverware. Set up your coffee-maker so you can simply press the "on" button in the morning. Bag lunches. Whatever you can do in thirty minutes at night will be thirty minutes less awaiting you in the morning when people aren't running at their best.

Keep it simple: While television may glamorize a gorgeous family sitting down to pancakes made in the shape of hearts, the practical parent knows the value of simplicity — cereal or toast and a fruit juice. Save time-consuming breakfasts for a weekend treat or assign one night a week as "breakfast for dinner" night.

Listen to the weather ahead of time to guide children in clothing choices.

Have children layout their clothes and pack their own lunches. This can be a good responsibility for a chore and reward system.

Place your keys and briefcase near the door before retiring for the evening. Make sure to always put these items in the same place.

Decide on the breakfast menu before going to bed the night before. Eat meals that require little preparation or clean up, such as hot and cold cereals.

Give "warnings" that the "bus is leaving" thirty minutes, fifteen minutes and five minute prior to departure to keep kids on track.

Make sure kids have clocks in their bedrooms to monitor time.

Take it one thing at a time: Instead of wrestling with getting both yourself and your children ready in the morning, get up an hour early so that you are dressed and showered before your children wake — and you've had time for a cup of coffee.

Encourage children's promptness with a mark on their reward chart. If you give allowance, let morning preparation be one of the responsibilities that helps children earn it.

If you have only one bathroom, prepare a bathroom schedule; let kids be responsible for getting in and out on time.

Your Assignment

Consider how the mornings in your home play out. Create a schedule that would work smoothly in your home. At minimum, implement at least one of the ideas from today's reading.

You may also choose to complete the "Designing Relaxing Evenings" worksheet that is included in the *Companion Workbook.*

YA step-by-step worksheet is also provided in the *Companion Workbook* for "customizing" your morning routine.

Day 47
Create a Space

✵

"The problem with the rat race is that
even if you win, you're still a rat."
Lily Tomlin

In our society, much emphasis has been placed on acquisition. We work to acquire this and that and constantly fill our lives with more and more "stuff." Even though some of us race to "gather the most toys," it is interesting to note that one of life's simplest joys is simplicity itself.

If you have an issue of *Architectural Digest,* or a different home magazine, glance through its pages. Find a spacious room or house. Notice how inviting this can be.

I think spaciousness is attractive since our lives are more packed than ever. Whether our days are filled with duties to-do or items to maintain, they have become overwhelmingly complex. Simplicity offers a space and freedom to escape from a crammed schedule.

Your Assignment

Choose a room (or an area within a room) to simplify. Make this area as basic as possible, discarding any extra clutter. Leave a few simple decorations. Over the next week, spend some regular time in this area each day. This simple exercise might help you change your thinking about “what to keep” and “what to toss,” and the “race to acquire more.”

Day 48
Ugly

"Do something every day that you don't want to-do; this is the golden rule for acquiring the habit of doing your duty without pain."
Mark Twain

Have you ever had one of those days (or weeks) where everything on your plate was something you didn't look forward to-doing? I faced such a week this past summer. I remember going to bed, doing my positive thinking, only to come face to face with the bleak reality that there wasn't one thing on my list I felt positive about. I had ended up with a pile of things I didn't really want to-do, but all the same had to be done.

Just before drifting off to sleep that Sunday night, I had an idea. I would make the upcoming week an "Ugly Week." Since I knew Monday contained three tasks I was dreading, I would find every other task I dreaded and fill the rest of the day. I would do the same thing for Tuesday and each other day that week. Every morning I would start with the task I *least* wanted to-do. The more annoying the task, the higher it would move on the priority list.

Monday morning came and I arose, determined to have my "Ugly Day." When the mail came, I didn't look at the fun stuff — just the bills. As I went throughout the day, I chose the tasks that went "against my grain." I worked through the backlog of unattractive to-dos.

By the end of the week, something interesting had happened. I had marked off so many of those "weigh one down" tasks that I was in an incredibly good mood and felt so much lighter.

When you find yourself in a backlog of to-dos that you don't want to-do, try this "ugly-week" tactic. Too often, we let these tasks remain undone and drain our energy for other tasks. When we incorporate just one "unattractive" task into our day, it can weigh us down the whole day. If we have twenty unattractive to-dos, we schedule ourselves for a month of "feeling under par." Having an "ugly week" allows us not only to consolidate those unattractive tasks, but also to feel good as we wipe the slate clean with "done" marks.

Intermission: Laughter

"You grow up the day you have
your first real laugh at yourself."
Ethel Barrymore

A couple of years ago, I remember sitting on my porch with several friends as the sun set, shooting brilliant rays of warm colors through an otherwise blue sky. It was during a season of life where my workload was more intense than it had ever been. Most of the work was by my own choosing; some of the work came from being a business owner and having to respond to different people or circumstances. My days average eighteen hours and I was fairly depleted — emotionally and physically.

I don't remember how exactly I ended up taking a break this particular evening, but I do know it was unplanned. Five of us enjoyed a drink while talking about anything that came to mind. Most of the company that evening was quite witty and soon our conversation turned to laughter — the kind that makes your stomach ache.

When everyone left that evening, I returned to my project — still smiling — an afterglow of the earlier laughter. I remember realizing that I had forgotten how good it felt to laugh. I missed that laughter. I missed the camaraderie.

Not only is laughing fun, there seems to be merit in the adage: "Laughter is the best medicine." A study by the center for preventive cardiology at the University of Maryland in Baltimore showed that those who laugh regularly are less likely to get heart disease. Another study published in *Journal of the American Medical Association*, showed that laughter increases the strength of the immune system.

At one point or another, we've all experienced the type of laughter that takes over our whole body. No matter how we try to stop it, another squeak or chuckle escapes. For a moment or two we are deliriously delivered "out of adulthood" into sheer fun and happiness. Laughter is waiting for us, but we won't find it if we don't look.

Consider laughter another vital nutrient to a healthy life. Incorporate activities that have you clutching your sides, into your life. Watch a video of a favorite comedian (I strongly suggest Steven Wright). Watch a comedy (the *Seinfeld* series is now on video) or try a movie (like *Liar, Liar*).

Part Eight

✵

Foundations of Financial Freedom

Days 48 and 49:

- ☐ Complete your gratitude journal each evening.
- ☐ Begin each day with a heartfelt "good morning."
- ☐ Carry your CATCH-ALL notebook with you everywhere.
- ☐ Transfer your to-do list each night.
- ☐ Complete your Nightly Reflection each evening.
- ☐ Each day, use the three-step action list.
- ☐ Consult your MASTER TASK LISTS for any other tasks that need to be completed.
- ☐ Do a daily laundry load if volume warrants.
- ☐ Host a daily "Happy Half-Hour."
- ☐ Practice the Five-Minute Relationship Miracle daily.
- ☐ Review your "value-card" daily.
- ☐ Give your children a self-esteem booster each day.
- ☐ Follow your morning routine.

Days 50 through 53:

- ☐ Complete your gratitude journal each evening.
- ☐ Begin each day with a heartfelt "good morning."
- ☐ Carry your CATCH-ALL notebook with you everywhere.
- ☐ Transfer your to-do list each night.
- ☐ Complete your Nightly Reflection each evening.
- ☐ Each day, use the three-step action list.
- ☐ Consult your MASTER TASK LISTS for any other tasks that need to be completed.
- ☐ Do a daily laundry load if volume warrants.
- ☐ Host a daily "Happy Half-Hour."
- ☐ Practice the Five-Minute Relationship Miracle daily.
- ☐ Review your "value-card" daily.
- ☐ Give your children a self-esteem booster each day.
- ☐ Follow your morning routine.
- ☐ Use your "value number" to evaluate all of your spending.

Day 49
Taking Stock

✵

"Plan your work and work your plan.
Decide in advance exactly how you are going to get
from where you are to where you want to go."
Brian Tracy

Janet Lackey, single parent of three-year-old Simon and five-year-old Jessica, dreads the two days each month that she sits down to pay bills. Janet is like 75 percent of US families, who according to Statistical Abstract of the United States, carry debt. Money problems need not be a major source of stress. You can build a solid financial plan — complete with investing tactics — to ease stress and take control of your finances. Money should be a gift — something to help us enjoy life, give to one another, and share. It shouldn't be a source of aggravation, tension, or fights. But when we don't control money, it tends to control us. In this part of the challenge we will look at how you can begin taking control of your finances. The first step to realizing permanent change is to take a "realistic snapshot" of where you are currently. Below, you'll find a simple yes or no evaluation that will allow you to see what areas you have conquered and what areas still need some work.

Taking Stock of Where You Are

1.Y N Do you have a monthly budget in place?

2.Y N Do you have a current will drawn up?

3.Y N Do you have a life insurance policy?

4.Y N Have you anticipated college costs for your children and made any preparations?

5. Y N Do you have an emergency savings fund established?

6. Y N Do you prepare your taxes on time and with ease?

7. Y N Is your checkbook balanced regularly?

8. Y N Have you begun saving for retirement, either through work or on your own?

9.Y N Do your family members have adequate health insurance coverage?

10. Y N Do you know where your credit rating stands?

11. Y N Have you investigated saving options besides a standard account to maximize your money's potential growth?

12. Y N Do your children understand the value and concept of money?

13. Y N Do you have adequate home (or renters) and auto insurance coverage?

Your Assignment

Complete the test above. In the upcoming days, we will examine how to conquer some of these common areas. Obviously, we can't "overhaul" your budget in a week, so like everything else in life, "choose your battles wisely." Take some time to look over the thirteen items and decide which are the major stressors for you. Circle your top three stressors and make those the first areas you tackle.

Day 49
Budgeting Basics

"The quickest way to-double your money is to fold it over and put it back in your pocket. "
Unkown

Emily Carr shares that "Although 99 percent of successful businesses in one survey regularly budgeted their expenditures, the same study showed that only sixty percent of individual consumers used budgets, and then only sporadically. You must learn to set up your household like a successful business." Like a business, households have receivables and payables, goals for the future, and current demands to meet.

Basic Budgeting in Three Simple Steps

Budgeting is basically a three-step process:

1. **Examine current spending habits**: Look through your receipts, checkbook register, and credit card statements to establish your personal spending categories.
2. **Set new spending goals**: Determine where you are overspending and project new spending goals for these categories. If you want to cut total spending by $200 per month, you should divvy "cutbacks" between several categories.

3. **Track your progress monthly:** Tabulate your receipts for each category and note how closely your actual spending is to your goals.

Without a budget, it's amazing how money can "disappear." I used to constantly have the debate with my mother about budgeting. I would keep asking her to budget her money and she would argue that there wasn't any money to budget. It's a chicken and egg circle. If you don't budget what you have, and begin working that budget, there will never be any extra money.

I use a basic budget worksheet, estimating my family's expenditures. I also learned to use cash and create an envelope system. Each week on Monday, I go to the bank and get cash for my husband, groceries, gas, our entertainment fund, and myself. I put these funds in envelopes labeled by category. Then, as we incur expenditures we use the cash from the applicable envelope. When the cash is gone, we quit spending. There is no easier way to stay out of debt than to quit spending when the cash is gone.

I also want to mention that keeping a budget is pointless *unless* you are going to analyze what happens each month. On the 31st, sit down and take a look at your spending. Did you stay within the desired ranges? If not, why? Do you need to re-evaluate your spending before next month? Did you under-estimate? Is there extra money? If so can you put it in savings?

There is no way around it — a budget is required to take you from point A to point B. Just like in business, when plans are made, companies work with the resources available to them to move from one goal to another. As you work to maximize your household's financial position, a budget will be the most important key.

To design a budget system, you'll need a folder with several pockets in which to organize all your forms and receipts. Forget the fancy budget books. I've tried enough of them to know that typically the expenses and layout aren't customizable for most families. It becomes more work than necessary. Instead, set out to make your own forms that are as basic as possible. This will give you a better chance at maintaining your budget system.

✎ Monthly worksheet templates are included in the *Companion Workbook*.

Designing the Monthly Worksheet

The easiest way to make a monthly worksheet is to divide your expenses into two categories, fixed expenses and variable expenses. List those expenses which you know to expect each month and whose cost does not vary. These might include rent or mortgage, car payment, insurance, utilities, *etc.* These will all be listed under "fixed expenses."

Under the variable expenses heading, list those items, which either vary month-to-month or are adjustable. These might include dry cleaning, groceries, phone bill, spending money, *etc.*

Taking a Realistic Look at What Your Budget Reveals

Once you have your budget in writing, take a moment to analyze what it reveals about your financial situation.

- If your income exceeds your expenses, is that money going into savings each month? If not, where is it going?
- Does your budget include life insurance, health insurance, anticipated college costs?
- Are there any categories that are receiving too much? Could you reduce any of the variable expenses without reducing the result? Instead of taking three children to a matinee, could a picnic be an ample and less expensive substitute?
- Compare what your budget reveals against the goals you wrote down earlier. Can you identify some of the basic steps to help you move toward these goals?

How to Maximize Your Budget

To optimize the effectiveness of your budget, track your expenses each month to make sure you are staying within the guidelines you have established. As you practice living within the guidelines of your budget, stay attentive for new options to save even more. Each month try to implement one or two new strategies for saving an extra five to ten dollars. Analyze your progress each month to make sure the budget is growing with your household. Re-figure as necessary.

Items on the Budget

The more specific your budget is, the better. Setup your budget to be as specific as you are comfortable. The more detailed the budget, the more you will be able to track your dollars and deduce extra opportunities for stashing savings.

Your Assignment

Create your own budgeting worksheet using today's guidelines. Or complete the budgeting worksheet in the *Change Your Life Challenge Workbook.*

Day 51
Change Your Thinking About Money

✵

"If you don't design your own life plan,
chances are you'll fall into someone else's plan.
And guess what they may have planned for you?
Not much."
Jim Rohn

One of the quickest ways to redo your finances it to change the way you think about money. For many, this simple exercise is as effective budgeting.

Think of money in terms of life's energy. This idea of taking your income, subtracting the cost of working, and dividing that number by the hours you work in a year is a concept developed by Vicki Robin, best-selling author of *Your Money or Your Life.*

Here is an example of how this works. Julie makes $26,000 a year gross. After taxes and her IRA she has $18,000 left. Day care totals $7280.00 annually. She commutes fifteen miles to work each way. At the government rate of .315 cents a mile, that's $2340.00 annually. Julie eats lunch out about twice a week and her average meals costs $7.00, to that we add two sodas and a coffee. These food expenses total $1170.00. Between dry cleaning, clothes, and pantyhose she spends an additional $960 each year.

Subtract these amounts from Julie's net income and she is left $6250.00 per year. Divide that by the 2000 hours she works and she is netting $3.12 per hour. *Knowing this number is the best way to spend less without budgeting.*

According to Robin you need to ask yourself, "Is this item worth this much of my life energy?" The next time you are looking at a $30.00 shirt, ask yourself, "Is this shirt worth ten hours (or six hours, or fourteen hours) of my time?" If it is, buy it. If it isn't, don't. Ask yourself this of everything you purchase.

Your Assignment

Today, figure out your own "value number." Begin by taking your annual gross income and then subtract the following (if you are married you can use your combined income):

Taxes
IRA or savings plans
Insurance
Day care
Dry cleaning expenses (associated with work)
Mileage driven per year (for work) x .32 a mile
Meals, sodas, or coffee purchased in conjunction with work
Divide your total by 2000 (or the number of hours that are worked to achieve your gross income)

The number derived is your "value" number. Use that in the future to evaluate your spending.

Day 51
Life Insurance

✵

"It's good to have money and the things
that money can buy, but it's good, too,
to check up once in a while and make sure you have-
n't lost the things that money can't buy."
George Horace Lorimer

Providing for children, in the event something should happen to us, is an important precautionary measure to take. All parents should have a will and life insurance. The following guidelines can steer you in a direction for life insurance coverage. (If you do not have children, you may choose to consider a life insurance policy that would cover the cost of funeral arrangements — however this may not be a financial priority. In that event, take the day off or work on another area of your finances.)

Deciding on the Amount of Coverage

To determine the coverage needed to provide ample care for your children, use the following formula:

1. Number of years income will need to be provided (typically until children reach an age to earn enough to support hemselves) ________
2. Estimated amount children will need each year ________

Multiply Amount in Question 1 by Question 2. ________

This provides an estimate of how much coverage will be needed.

Types of Policies

Term: The most economical of coverage. You pay a yearly premium for a specific death benefit. The premium increases with age.

Whole: While more expensive than term, this policy builds cash value and may also be borrowed against. Additionally, the premium is fixed for the full life of the policy, protecting the consumer against increases.

Universal Life: Is a newer form of insurance that allows more flexibility than the previous options. Your death benefit, cash value, and length of premium payments can vary over the years. You can also raise or lower both the death benefit and the premiums throughout your life. These policies are, however, interest sensitive.

Variable Life: Another, newer policy where you can choose the investment options for your premium. While these do provide life insurance along with investment options, their appropriateness depends on your financial circumstances.

Your Assignment

Using this knowledge as a springboard, contact a local life insurance agent to see how the different types of policies can benefit your family. You may find that you can't jump in with a policy that equals the total amount needed. That's fine. Start where you can. Never be shy about investigating your options. People want to help you. You can also search for life insurance online and obtain rates and quotes over the Internet.

In addition to life insurance, everyone (especially those with children under eighteen) should have a valid and current will. If you do not have such a document, tucked in a safe place, make a short-term goal to create one. There are many "kits" available today that make this process simple and easy. If you choose to use a kit, make sure that the kit complies with the laws of your state.

Day 53

Final Thoughts on Finance

"Find something you love to-do
and you'll never have to work a day in your life."
Harvey Mackay

While we could explore finance forever, I want to offer basic tools in this phase of the challenge that will help you get your financial house in order. Use this information as a springboard to take control.

I am providing some resources that I feel are extremely valuable for when you are ready to explore and learn more about budgeting. Choose one or two to explore further in the upcoming weeks.

COMPOUNDING: CHALLENGE YOURSELF TO SAVE

http://www.free-financial-advice.net/compounding-effect.html

This page focuses on the effect of COMPOUNDING. I'm sure you've heard over and over again about how money can grow so rapidly over time. This is one of the best pages I have found that truly explains how compounding works and its benefits. I really urge each of you to challenge yourself to put some money away in a plan like this — even if it's only several dollars each week.

CREDIT CARD DEBT: CHALLENGE YOURSELF TO BREAK FREE

http://www.free-financial-advice.net/credit-card-debt.html

http://www.free-financial-advice.net/consolidate-debt.html

These links offer advice for consolidating debt and also include links and explanations of many services that can help you.

THE STOCK MARKET: CHALLENGE YOURSELF TO INVEST

http://www.free-financial-advice.net/stock-market.html

Even in uncertain financial times, the stock market remains a good option for multiplying your dollars. Many people shy away from the stock market thinking they need to have thousands of dollars to invest. Not so. The link above will give you a basic "stock market primer." When I began thinking about investing in the stock market, I started by choosing stocks and building a "fake" portfolio (I didn't really buy the stock). I did this for several months so I could see what would have happened and how I would have faired. When I felt comfortable with my results I started using real money. One warning: Make sure the stocks you investigate match your risk-tolerance. I tend to have a very risky personality and buy high-risk stocks — meaning sometimes I make a lot, but other times I lose a lot. Look at a stock's history before purchasing to make sure the best-case scenario and the worst-case scenario are both scenarios you can stomach. Never invest more than you can afford to lose.

Your Assignment

Choose one of the above financial areas to explore further. Record the area in either your SHORT-TERM or LONG-TERM project list.

Intermission: Forgiveness

"The important thing to remember when it comes to forgiving is that forgiveness doesn't make the other person right; it makes you free."
Stormie Omartian

How do we know if we need to forgive someone, something, or even ourselves? We know because we feel a gnawing sadness inside of us, although we may not know the cause.

The interesting thing about choosing not to forgive, is that it hurts us more than anyone else. Your inability to forgive anything or anyone in your world may hurt someone else a bit, but I guarantee it hurts you and your world a hundred times more.

As a visual example, think of two goal posts set twenty-feet apart. A more content and peaceful life rests just after the goal posts — all you have to-do is run through the twenty-foot space, blindfolded and voila, you will be closer to the life you want. It will be a little tough, granted your are blindfolded — but there is a big enough area where you should be able to break through to the other side with a few attempts. Unforgiveness is like an eighteen-foot wall. Place that between your goal posts and now try running toward that other side. Maybe you'll get through. Most likely, you'll get some bad bruises, or maybe a broken bone, and probably give up, believing that there really isn't a space — just a brick wall. Like a wall, unforgiveness blocks our path.

Forgiveness Brings Freedom

An unforgiving nature is very costly in our lives. We may find ourselves attaching to other people in unhealthy ways, punishing other people, or losing hope in the world and in our peers.

The first step in forgiveness is to understand all the elements of the incident we are trying to forgive. We may be forgiving God, a person who harmed or hurt us, or a person who has harmed or hurt someone we love. We may be forgiving our parents, our society, our world, or ourselves. Forgiveness does not mean that we are condoning hurtful actions. It doesn't mean that we accept inappropriate actions of others. Forgiveness does not mean that we forget how much we hurt. Forgiveness simply means that we acknowledge the deep pain we feel, but choose to move past that pain. We forgive those who contributed to our pain and let their actions become part of our past. We let go.

We can dislike what someone has done to us, but we can still forgive them and allow them to be someone new, instead of freeze-framing them in that hurtful place.

Sometimes looking at this in a different perspective can be extremely helpful. Think back and recall a time when you did something hurtful to someone. Perhaps you said something "off the cuff " that hurt someone's feelings, or perhaps you did something you were ashamed about. Take a few moments to recollect the most vivid example that you can. Now think through the series of events that led up to your action. You did something hurtful and how did the other person respond? Did they eventually forgive you? What would happen if they hadn't? What would happen if the person had stayed angry at you for that action? You made a mistake, a bad decision, or didn't think before acting, and if they didn't forgive you, they would never be able to see you how you are now. Unforgiveness chains people to their painful actions and pasts. We freeze that painful time. Can you see how that person would be missing all you could offer? Or how that person could become so focused on the pain you caused, that they would miss the other good happening around them?

A classic example is the spiteful lover. You have probably met someone like this or have seen a likeness depicted in a movie. They have been "wronged" somehow in a relationship and have become adamant that the opposite sex is "not worthy of their time." Instead of realizing they had a painful experience, acknowledging it and moving on, they continually focus on their pain. Meanwhile, one thousand perfect matches could walk right by and they would never know. They are too busy focusing on life's injustices. Many friendships end this way. There is some fight or spat between close friends or neighbors, and instead of practicing forgiveness, people practice grudge-holding. Eventually, hearts grow bitter and less trusting.

At one point in my life, I was so concerned with how others saw me. I wanted to make sure everyone had the actual facts on which to base their thoughts and opinions. If someone held what I perceived to be an unfair view, I would go to great lengths to get my own "evidence" into their hands or to defend myself. I cannot tell you how exhausting this was. Liberation came when I made the decision to truly "let go." I began to focus only on blessing others — no matter what they thought of me. I quit trying to "present my case" and instead began to "live my life." Everyday I set out to live the best life, and do the best work I am capable of doing. I will let that action speak for itself.

Forgiveness means to "give as before." To quote John Bradshaw from his book *The Family*, "It means that we give up resentments and release the energy that has kept us in bondage."

Think about an event where you have not forgiven someone. Write down what emotions you feel when you recall that event. Now think back to a time before that event happened. Did you feel these emotions? You probably did not. When you forgive, you give yourself the freedom to let go of the hurtful emotions and enjoy the positive that can be found. When there aren't any positives to be found, forgiveness gives us permission to let go, move forward and grow.

Even when we have been able to forgive those who have hurt us, we often cannot forgive ourselves. Many of us unfairly hold ourselves prisoner to unrealistic standards that we would never expect of another person. Patricia Commins writes, "self-love is the only way to move forward. It is the only cure for the wounds of the soul, the only escape route from the negative patterns of the past."

Self-Forgiveness Reality Check Exercise

Recall an incident for which you have not forgiven yourself. Write about the incident in your journal. Now close your eyes. Imagine a morning where you are sitting in your kitchen with a cup of coffee one morning when a dear friend knocks at your door. Your friend is trying to hold back her tears, but you know she has been crying from her tear-stained face.

You invite her in and she crumbles into the chair across from you. When you ask what is wrong, she bursts into tears, mumbling her story of sadness through strained breath. Imagine that her story of sadness is the same or parallel to the event recorded in your journal. Visualize yourself advising your friend. What do you say? Do you make her feel worse, by amplifying her mistake? Do you lecture her, implying she should hold herself hostage to her mistake and let it cause unhappiness throughout her life? Or do you take a different tactic? Take a moment to thoroughly visualize your response, and then write about it in your journal.

A true friend would not let another friend suffer indefinitely — even for the worst of actions. Instead, a true friend would suggest accountability while encouraging self-forgiveness and forward movement. Try offering yourself that same wisdom.

Try another quick visualization. This time imagine it is you who is crying at the table. Take the same attitude with which you responded to your friend, and apply it to your situation. Write out the council you receive in your journal. Try this exercise whenever you feel you are being unforgiving of yourself.

Simple Self-Love Exercise

For those of us who have not practiced self-love, it can be a difficult concept to grasp. Begin with a simple gesture of self-directed love. Perhaps it is five minutes of uninterrupted reading, or a hot bubble bath, or a walk in nature, or meeting a friend for a cup of coffee. It can be anything that validates the importance of treating yourself well. Create a list in your journal of simple ways you can express self-love. Affirm your value daily by practicing one of these exercises.

Part Nine

To Your Health

Day 54

- ☐ Complete your gratitude journal each evening.
- ☐ Begin each day with a heartfelt "good morning."
- ☐ Carry your CATCH-ALL notebook with you everywhere.
- ☐ Transfer your to-do list each night.
- ☐ Complete your Nightly Reflection each evening.
- ☐ Each day, use the three-step action list.
- ☐ Consult your MASTER TASK LISTS for any other tasks that need to be completed.
- ☐ Do a daily laundry load if volume warrants.
- ☐ Host a daily "Happy Half-Hour."
- ☐ Practice the Five-Minute Relationship Miracle daily.
- ☐ Review your "value-card" daily.
- ☐ Give your children a self-esteem booster each day.
- ☐ Follow your morning routine.
- ☐ Use your "value number" to evaluate all of your spending.
- ☐ Drink at least eight, (8 oz.) glasses of water today.

Day 55

- ☐ Complete your gratitude journal each evening.
- ☐ Begin each day with a heartfelt "good morning."
- ☐ Carry your CATCH-ALL notebook with you everywhere.
- ☐ Transfer your to-do list each night.
- ☐ Complete your Nightly Reflection each evening.
- ☐ Each day, use the three-step action list.
- ☐ Consult your MASTER TASK LISTS for any other tasks that need to be completed.
- ☐ Do a daily laundry load if volume warrants.
- ☐ Host a daily "Happy Half-Hour."
- ☐ Practice the Five-Minute Relationship Miracle daily.
- ☐ Review your "value-card" daily.
- ☐ Give your children a self-esteem booster each day.
- ☐ Follow your morning routine.
- ☐ Use your "value number" to evaluate all of your spending.
- ☐ Drink at least eight, (8 oz.) glasses of water today.
- ☐ Incorporate your "starting level" of daily exercise.

Day 56

☐ Complete your gratitude journal each evening.
☐ Begin each day with a heartfelt "good morning."
☐ Carry your CATCH-ALL notebook with you everywhere.
☐ Transfer your to-do list each night.
☐ Complete your Nightly Reflection each evening.
☐ Each day, use the three-step action list.
☐ Consult your MASTER TASK LISTS for any other tasks that need to be completed.
☐ Do a daily laundry load if volume warrants.
☐ Host a daily "Happy Half-Hour."
☐ Practice the Five-Minute Relationship Miracle daily.
☐ Review your "value-card" daily.
☐ Give your children a self-esteem booster each day.
☐ Follow your morning routine.
☐ Use your "value number" to evaluate all of your spending.
☐ Drink at least eight, (8 oz.) glasses of water today.
☐ Incorporate your "starting level" of daily exercise.
☐ Have a healthy breakfast.

Days 57 and 58

☐ Complete your gratitude journal each evening.
☐ Begin each day with a heartfelt "good morning."
☐ Carry your CATCH-ALL notebook with you everywhere.
☐ Transfer your to-do list each night.
☐ Complete your Nightly Reflection each evening.
☐ Each day, use the three-step action list.
☐ Consult your MASTER TASK LISTS for any other tasks that need to be completed.
☐ Do a daily laundry load if volume warrants.
☐ Host a daily "Happy Half-Hour."
☐ Practice the Five-Minute Relationship Miracle daily.
☐ Review your "value-card" daily.
☐ Give your children a self-esteem booster each day.
☐ Follow your morning routine.
☐ Use your "value number" to evaluate all of your spending.

☐ Drink at least eight, (8 oz.) glasses of water today.
☐ Incorporate your "starting level" of daily exercise.
☐ Have a healthy breakfast.
☐ Add some fruit and veggies to your meals today.

Day 59

☐ Complete your gratitude journal each evening.
☐ Begin each day with a heartfelt "good morning."
☐ Carry your CATCH-ALL notebook with you everywhere.
☐ Transfer your to-do list each night.
☐ Complete your Nightly Reflection each evening.
☐ Each day, use the three-step action list.
☐ Consult your MASTER TASK LISTS for any other tasks that need to be completed.
☐ Do a daily laundry load if volume warrants.
☐ Host a daily "Happy Half-Hour."
☐ Practice the Five-Minute Relationship Miracle daily.
☐ Review your "value-card" daily.
☐ Give your children a self-esteem booster each day.
☐ Follow your morning routine.
☐ Use your "value number" to evaluate all of your spending.
☐ Drink at least eight, (8 oz.) glasses of water today.
☐ Incorporate your "starting level" of daily exercise.
☐ Have a healthy breakfast.
☐ Add some fruit and veggies to your meals today.
☐ Eat all of your meals and snacks at the table.

Day 54
The Water Rule

✵

"To insure good health: Eat lightly, breathe deeply,
live moderately, cultivate cheerfulness,
and maintain an interest in life."
William Londen

In this phase of the challenge, we are going to focus on our physical wellness. Even though we know we need to be healthy in order to meet daily demands, taking care of ourselves is the most commonly ignored area.

We know we *should* take care of ourselves — but when we are bouncing from crisis to crisis we often have to cut something out of our lives and nine times out of ten, we cut self-care.

When we repeatedly cut self-care, we find ourselves easily fatigued, depressed, or in "a funk." Yet we feel selfish taking valuable time and spending it on ourselves. I'm here to tell you that this is one of the biggest stigmas we need to overcome. If we don't take care of our most valuable asset — ourselves — we simply cannot be at our best or take care of others. End of story. It's not selfish — in fact it's just the opposite. It is only selfish if you ignore yourself, assuming you'll always "be there" to take care of others, without taking care of yourself. In fact, that's selfish *and* irresponsible.

I know how highly engrained these messages are, so I am not going to suggest that you implement huge overnight changes. I'm not going to ask you to omit anything from your life, either. If you want to eat bon-bons by the pound — go for it. Instead, I am going to ask you to take a few significant steps to dramatically improve your wellness. My one request is that you complete these assignments in ADDITION to eating your pound of bon-bons (or any other unhealthy behavior). I hope you will find, as I did, that when you complete the simple steps herein, you will be less drawn to unhealthy habits. You won't have to "force" yourself to give them up — you'll give them up naturally — and without cravings.

You have undoubtedly heard that we need to drink six to eight, 8-ounce glasses of water each day. Studies have shown that most of us are walking around dehydrated. Dehydration leads to fatigue, depression, and food cravings — amongst a bunch of other not-so-healthy conditions.

HOW TO ACHIEVE ADEQUATE WATER INTAKE:

Drink 8 oz. upon waking
Drink 8 oz. before breakfast
Drink 8 oz. before lunch
Drink 8 oz. with lunch
Drink 8 oz. in the afternoon
Drink 8 oz. before dinner
Drink 8 oz. with dinner

In case you were wondering, caffinated drinks do not count (like coffee or tea). In fact, for each caffi-

nated drink you consume, many studies recommend you increase your water intake by eight ounces.

I like to use liter-size water bottles. Each night before I go to bed, I fill the bottles up with my needed water intake for the following day. Throughout the day I drink (and drink and drink).

Your Assignment

Have you guessed what your daily assignment is? Choose whatever method you wish but get that water in! If you want a bonus challenge — try doing this at least five days a week for three weeks and watch what happens. Your skin will glow, you will feel healthier, and the amount of not-so-good fluids you drink will decrease without other effort (soda, coffee, *etc.*). Just as you carry your CATCH-ALL notebook with you, make a habit of carrying a bottle of water.

✎ There is a worksheet for tracking water and food groups in the *Companion Workbook.*

Day 55
Let's Get Moving

✵

"If you are seeking creative ideas, go out walking. Angels whisper to a man when he goes for a walk."
Raymond Inmon

Now that you are hydrated — let's get moving. Don't worry — there isn't any high-intensity, kick-boxing, step-jumping required. (Although if you like high-intensity cardio activities, I encourage you to engage in them.)

For the purpose of this program, all we are going to look at is a twenty-minute walk, five days a week. (You don't have to start at twenty minutes, you can work up to it.) Put on a pair of comfortable athletic shoes, head out the door, and walk for ten minutes. Then turn around and walk back.

If you don't have a block of twenty minutes, then do ten minutes in the morning and ten more at night. If you don't have two increments of ten minutes — you need to go back to Day Ten and read the PRESCRIPTION FOR PROCRASTINATION. If the president can make time for daily exercise, you can too. It's likely not a matter of time — but desire.

Try and change your thinking about exercise. Consider it a ten-minute escape into nature. Or consider it twenty minutes for you to think about whatever you want — outside of the demands everyone places on you. Or think of it as something as important to your overall health as brushing your teeth. You *need* this to become a daily habit.

My assistant, MaryAnn, is a great example of a person who incorporated exercise as part of her life. MaryAnn has battled with her weight all her life and this past spring she truly *committed* and truly *desired* lasting change. She has used liquid diets in the past that had helped her lose one-hundred pounds — only to gain it back plus more. She was no longer looking for the quick fix — she was out for lasting change. She and I started exercise regimens around the same time. My goal was a three-mile walk or run every day, working up to ten and fifteen mile walks and runs so I could complete my first 26.2 marathon in the fall. MaryAnn's goal? Walk five minutes. Guess what happened?

I quickly became frustrated. I could never find the time to run three miles and when I did I was tired and achy. MaryAnn, however, walked five minutes on her lunch break. After two weeks, she changed her goal to seven minutes. Now, several months later, MaryAnn walks thirty to sixty minutes every day like clockwork. (For those of you trying to figure out how far that would be, ironically, it's about three miles.) Where did I end up? Abandoning my marathon plan and starting at the beginning like MaryAnn did. She is a true example of how step-by-step, minute-by-minute, we can change our habits and head toward a better life.

Your Assignment

Decide whether you will walk:

1. One 20-minute segment

2. Two 10-minute segments

3. Four 5-minute segments

Decide when during the day you will walk.

Decide which five days per week you will do it. (If five days seems like too many, start with three and work up to five over the next six weeks.) Write these appointments in pen on your calendar. Grab your walking shoes and get moving!

 There is a worksheet for tracking exercise in the *Companion Workbook.*

Day 56
Time for Breakfast

"We are what we repeatedly do.
Excellence, then, is not an act, but a habit."
Aristotle

I am a habitual breakfast-skipper. I am never hungry in the morning, so I tend to just ignore breakfast all together. Many times I'm not hungry at lunch either — and then somewhere around late afternoon I suddenly feel like I am going to pass-out if I don't consume a meal the size of Texas. I won't recite the research, because I am sure you know it already: Breakfast is the most important meal of the day.

But what you may not know is that *what* you consume for breakfast and *when* you consume it can dramatically affect your functionality throughout the day.

Our metabolisms are sluggish when we wake and having something to eat within an hour helps our metabolism begin functioning for a productive day. Recently, I read that the longer we go without food, the harder it is to get our metabolisms to function at maximum efficiency. In fact if we haven't eaten by noon, we may as well forget a super-effective metabolism for the day.

When I decided to change my ways and eat breakfast, I was hopeful that the sluggishness I felt in the afternoon would go away. I ate one to two bowls of whole-grain cereal and waited in anticipation for my Super-Woman cape to magically appear. Nothing happened.

Upon further research, I learned that I was, like many Americans, eating way too many carbs, and skimping on protein. Although the whole-wheat cereal I was eating was very healthy — it wasn't a *balanced* meal. I don't subscribe to the Atkins plan (although I have no problem with those who do) but upon evaluating my diet, I discovered I had plenty of carbs and not enough protein. So I changed my breakfast to be an egg, over medium, with a slice of wheat toast.

To explain it in a simplified way, when we eat carbs we release quick-acting energy — we get an immediate "boost." But when the carbs wear off, we begin to sag. (That is why so many people have recommended we eat smaller meals throughout the day — by doing that we can better maintain our blood sugar and an even metabolism.) Proteins, however, release slowly and provide a more long-lasting form of energy. In summary, we need both carbs and proteins to keep our body running at maximum power. When we use just one of these food-fuels we are like a car trying to run on just gas or just oil . It doesn't work (or at least not for long).

Your Assignment

Whatever your excuse, toss it out the window. Sit down and plan out a week's worth of breakfast menus that balance carbs and protein. Try to eat your breakfast within one hour of waking for maximum metabolism benefit.

Simple Speedy Breakfast Solutions: *Smoothies are super fast — however, if you are going to use the excuse that you don't even have time to make a smoothie in the morning, then try one of the many* ***MEAL REPLACEMENT BARS*** *on the market today. I personally like* ***THE ZONE*** *bars (strawberry-yogurt) and the* ***SLIM-FAST*** *(chocolate-chip) bars. I have also included my personal creation, the Rush Hour Smoothie®.*

Here is my breakfast invention that offers a way to get the majority of your daily RDA met in a single meal.

The Rush Hour Cook's Morning Smoothie

1 cup frozen berries of your choice
½ frozen banana (peel bananas, split in half, wrap in foil and freeze. This is a great way to use brown bananas. They still taste great in a smoothie!
½ cup nonfat plain yogurt
½ cup orange juice (more or less depending on the consistency you like)
2 tablespoons flax seed*
1 tablespoon organic greens*
1 scoop whey protein powder (vanilla flavored)*
Combine all ingredients in a blender and mix well.

*These ingredients can be purchased at health supply stores and GNC® www.gnc.com They are all optional ingredients, but part of the key component to meeting your RDA.)

This is a great morning snack for kids, too! They taste so rich and Creamy — it's like having a delicious berry shake!

The Rush Hour Cook Club

If you haven't joined already make sure to stop by www.rushhourcook.com and join our free cooking club. You'll enjoy prizes, contests, and more recipes delivered to your in-box Monday through Friday.

Day 57
Add Some Fruit and Veggies

"Tell me what you eat,
and I will tell you what you are."
Anthelme Brillat-Savarin

Let's look at another quick and easy way to dramatically improve your health. Before we begin, here is some background reading from the Department of Health:

It has been estimated that diet might contribute to the development of one-third of all cancers, and that increasing fruit and vegetable consumption is the second most important cancer prevention strategy, after reducing smoking. In 1998, the Department of Health's Committee on Medical Aspects of Food Policy and Nutrition reviewed the evidence and concluded that higher vegetable consumption would reduce the risk of ***colorectal cancer*** *and* ***gastric cancer****. There was also weakly consistent evidence that higher fruit and vegetable consumption would reduce the risk of* ***breast cancer****. These cancers combined represent about eighteen percent of the cancer burden in men and about thirty percent in women. Research suggests that there are other health benefits too, including delaying the development of* ***cataracts****, reducing the* *symptoms of* ***asthma****, improving bowel function, and helping to* ***manage diabetes****.*

Those are some pretty amazing statistics aren't they? And in addition to all those benefits, eating fruits and veggies increases fiber intake, vitamins, and helps weight loss efforts. We should have at least five servings of fruits and veggies each day. If you eat few vegetables or fruits, ramping intake to five-a-day may seem impossible. Then start slow. If you have one or less servings per day, aim for one to two servings per day. If you currently have one or two — then aim for two to three servings. Keep gradually increasing your consumption until you hit five-a-day at least six days each week.

In my aim to consume five to six servings of fruit and vegetables each day, I asked my nutritionist if I should be concerned with how many servings were fruits and how many were vegetables. She said that it did not matter. While it was good to have some from each group, whether I was a fruit-fanatic or only ate vegetables, I could still chalk it up as "mission accomplished.'

Your Assignment

Here are some easy ways to add more fruits and veggies to your diet. Begin today by implementing at least one of these strategies.

- Choose one snack a day to replace with a fruit or vegetable. (Try carrots or broccoli with a reduced-fat ranch dressing. celery and natural peanut butter, an apple, or a banana.)
- Start your day with a fresh-fruit smoothie made from 1/2 cup fat free yogurt, frozen fruit, and orange juice for desired consistency. Or you can use fresh fruit and ice instead of frozen fruit)
- Each day toss a banana or apple in your purse and munch it down at some point during the day.
- Always serve a side salad with lunch and dinner.
- Always serve a steamed vegetable with dinner.
- Serve fruit salad topped with yogurt and granola for breakfast. Make a bit extra and you can grab a second fruit serving as a mid-day snack.

OTHER TIPS: Buy vegetables that are ready-to-eat like skinned, baby carrots or carrot chips, already-washed spring greens, precut melon and fruit. Often the number one bandit, robbing us of the health benefit of these foods, is PREPARATION TIME! Prepared foods help conquer this nemesis.

Pick up an apple corer. These are great! Just rinse your apple and press the corer down on top. It removes the core and seeds and leaves your apple in ready-to-eat slices.

Day 58
Find a Wellness Community

✵

"Take care of your body with steadfast fidelity. The soul must see through these eyes alone, and if they are dim, the whole world is clouded."
Johann Wolfgang von Goethe

Time and time again I have seen how challenges backed by a support group are accomplished more often than when people "go it alone." Having a few people to fall back on when we face hardships, have questions, or just need a word of encouragement can really make the difference in our attempts to create lasting change.

One woman who has been vital in helping me with healthy habits is Carrie Myers Smith, author of *Squeezing Your Size 14 Self Into A Size 6 World: A real-woman's guide to food, fitness and self-acceptance* (Champion Press, 2004). Carrie taught me how to take simple and realistic steps. I quit making *huge* life leaps that set me up for failure. Instead I tackled one mini-goal at a time. She helped me give up the word *diet* and understand the true meaning, purpose, and benefits of a healthy life-long eating plan.

Carrie has brought her coaching and tips to the Internet and you can enjoy a free membership to her WOMEN IN WELLNESS site. Check it out for lots of great ideas, tools, and a support community to encourage you in any health goal.

Your Assignment

Log on to www.womeninwellness.com and browse the free support offerings and classes. Consider joining this support community, or create your own with two or three friends.

Day 59
The Simplest Diet in the World

✵

"In two decades I've lost a total of 789 pounds. I should be hanging from a charm bracelet."
Erma Bombeck

Recently, our family began seeing a nutritionist. My daughter's eating habits weren't that great (neither were mine nor my husband's for that matter) and we desired professional direction. I had a ten-year history with an eating disorder. Although I had not engaged in eating-disordered behaviors for some time, I often skipped meals or did not make the healthiest choices. When my daughter became interested in nutrition and started asking questions left and right, I decided a nutritionist would be the best choice for answers.

I found that our nutritionist is one of the most down-to-earth women I have ever met. Her approaches are simple, realistic, and healthy for both body and mind. Our assignment for the first month was quite simple and contained three parts.

The first was one we covered briefly in an earlier day. Eat within sixty minutes of waking. Her definition of a meal is that it must contain at least three food groups. She encourages three meals a day plus snacks (and snacks must contain two food groups.) Using this format, we feel "full" more often and less likely to make unhealthy choices.

The second part of our assignment was to spend two hours per week engaged in a physical family activity. She suggested we use our membership at the YMCA and go swim together or play a game of basketball.

The third part of our assignment, and the one that caused the most change for us, was to eat absolutely everything at the dining room table. No more eating in the living room or eating while watching television or eating at the computer. Every meal and snack had to be consumed while sitting at the table. While eating, one has to focus just on the food — no reading the paper or skimming a magazine.

This third step dramatically changed our family's food intake. We became conscious of our food choices. Those family members who tended to eat more than their allotted servings — stopped. It is hard to sit at a table and just eat a bag of chips.

The "play" component was also interesting. In the past, I tended to put off exercise because it was one more demand that took away from my "family time." The nutritionist's exercise- requirement was not only fun, but increased family time.

As I thought about the assignment, I realized what the nutritionist was doing. Her approach is similar to that of the challenge. The biggest obstacle to implementation is trying to change too many things at once. We try to "overhaul" what we are eating, while also finding time to make these changes. She realized that if she could get us to change a few basic habits for how we spend our time, then she could change what we do with that time later.

For example, once she has us all eating at the table regularly, we can focus more on our food choices. Once she has us regularly carving out a few hours each week for physical activity, she can change the demands of our physical activity. First, she is having us commit to creating the time for change. Once we have completed that task, she will focus on how we spend that time. It is a simple, realistic approach to change in today's hectic world.

Meanwhile, as we worked toward our changes, I was amazed how simple the act of sitting at a table for all food consumption dramatically changed everyone's consciousness of what and when they were eating. That one step allowed my family to take incredible strides toward improved health.

Your Assignment

Begin eating every meal and snack at the table. Set that as a new family rule. (Beverages are excluded; they can be consumed in any area of the home.) Begin the process of eliminating "absent-minded" eating.

Part Ten

✵

Taking Care of Yourself While Taking Care of Everyone Else

Daily Action List

Day 60

- ☐ Complete your gratitude journal each evening.
- ☐ Begin each day with a heartfelt "good morning."
- ☐ Carry your CATCH-ALL notebook with you everywhere.
- ☐ Transfer your to-do list each night.
- ☐ Complete your Nightly Reflection each evening.
- ☐ Each day, use the three-step action list.
- ☐ Consult your MASTER TASK LISTS for any other tasks that need to be completed.
- ☐ Do a daily laundry load if volume warrants.
- ☐ Host a daily "Happy Half-Hour."
- ☐ Practice the Five-Minute Relationship Miracle daily.
- ☐ Review your "value-card" daily.
- ☐ Give your children a self-esteem booster each day.
- ☐ Follow your morning routine.
- ☐ Use your "value number" to evaluate all of your spending.
- ☐ Drink at least eight, (8 oz.) glasses of water today.
- ☐ Incorporate your "starting level" of daily exercise.
- ☐ Have a healthy breakfast.
- ☐ Add some fruit and veggies to your meals today.
- ☐ Eat all of your meals and snacks at the table.

Day 61

- ☐ Complete your gratitude journal each evening.
- ☐ Begin each day with a heartfelt "good morning."
- ☐ Carry your CATCH-ALL notebook with you everywhere.
- ☐ Transfer your to-do list each night.
- ☐ Complete your Nightly Reflection each evening.
- ☐ Each day, use the three-step action list.
- ☐ Consult your MASTER TASK LISTS for any other tasks that need to be completed.

- ☐ Do a daily laundry load if volume warrants.
- ☐ Host a daily "Happy Half-Hour."
- ☐ Practice the Five-Minute Relationship Miracle daily.
- ☐ Review your "value-card" daily.
- ☐ Give your children a self-esteem booster each day.
- ☐ Follow your morning routine.
- ☐ Use your "value number" to evaluate all of your spending.
- ☐ Drink at least eight, (8 oz.) glasses of water today.
- ☐ Incorporate your "starting level" of daily exercise.
- ☐ Have a healthy breakfast.
- ☐ Add some fruit and veggies to your meals today.
- ☐ Eat all of your meals and snacks at the table.
- ☐ Choose a "Personal Power Card" to carry with you daily.

Day 62

- ☐ Complete your gratitude journal each evening.
- ☐ Begin each day with a heartfelt "good morning."
- ☐ Carry your CATCH-ALL notebook with you everywhere.
- ☐ Transfer your to-do list each night.
- ☐ Complete your Nightly Reflection each evening.
- ☐ Each day, use the three-step action list.
- ☐ Consult your MASTER TASK LISTS for any other tasks that need to be completed.
- ☐ Do a daily laundry load if volume warrants.
- ☐ Host a daily "Happy Half-Hour."
- ☐ Practice the Five-Minute Relationship Miracle daily.
- ☐ Review your "value-card" daily.
- ☐ Give your children a self-esteem booster each day.
- ☐ Follow your morning routine.
- ☐ Use your "value number" to evaluate all of your spending.
- ☐ Drink at least eight, (8 oz.) glasses of water today.
- ☐ Incorporate your "starting level" of daily exercise.
- ☐ Have a healthy breakfast.
- ☐ Add some fruit and veggies to your meals today.
- ☐ Eat all of your meals and snacks at the table.
- ☐ Choose a "Personal Power Card" to carry with you daily.
- ☐ Take at least one ten-minute retreat today.

Days 63 through 66

- ☐ Complete your gratitude journal each evening.
- ☐ Begin each day with a heartfelt "good morning."
- ☐ Carry your CATCH-ALL notebook with you everywhere.
- ☐ Transfer your to-do list each night.
- ☐ Complete your Nightly Reflection each evening.
- ☐ Each day, use the three-step action list.
- ☐ Consult your MASTER TASK LISTS for any other tasks that need to be completed.
- ☐ Do a daily laundry load if volume warrants.
- ☐ Host a daily "Happy Half-Hour."
- ☐ Practice the Five-Minute Relationship Miracle daily.
- ☐ Review your "value-card" daily.
- ☐ Give your children a self-esteem booster each day.
- ☐ Follow your morning routine.
- ☐ Use your "value number" to evaluate all of your spending.
- ☐ Drink at least eight, (8 oz.) glasses of water today.
- ☐ Incorporate your "starting level" of daily exercise.
- ☐ Have a healthy breakfast.
- ☐ Add some fruit and veggies to your meals today.
- ☐ Eat all of your meals and snacks at the table.
- ☐ Choose a "Personal Power Card" to carry with you daily.
- ☐ Take at least one ten-minute retreat today.
- ☐ Visualize tomorrow before going to sleep tonight.

Day 60
Nurturing Yourself

✵

"How many cares one loses when one decides not to be something, but to be someone."
Coco Chanel

While working on two books, establishing a business and raising my two-year-old, my days were always too short, and my stress level was at its peak. The demands on my time were great and the first thing to go, to make room for these demands, was my daily walk. The second thing to go was home-cooked meals. The third thing I shaved from my day was two hours of sleep. For a month or two this worked well, but then the hectic pace and lack of balance caught up with me. I felt I had no choice. To meet the demands that were bombarding my life, I had to find more time and that meant less time for myself. Didn't it? As I relayed this frustration to a friend, he questioned my priorities and the lack of "me time" in my schedule. I informed him that I simply had no choice. I had taken on these commitments and had to make the time for them. Yet he noticed my voice was monotone, and my typical excitement toward my endeavors was evaporating. He offered suggestion after suggestion, and I countered each with the same reason: I would feel guilty doing so much for myself when there was so much else that needed tending. Finally, he offered the following anecdote.

"Your house is on fire. You're on the way to an important presentation. You're late, and the deadline is one that could cost you great consequence. But you look back, and there is that house burning. Everything you treasured in your life succumbing to flames. The fire is moving slowly enough that you could get out some of your most prized possessions — family photos, memories — of course, this will only make you later for your presentation. What do you do?"

I rolled my eyes. This seemed like an obvious choice. "I'd go back," I replied. "I'm not crazy enough to let all that go, over some meeting."

"Would you feel guilty for doubling back?"

"No," I said immediately.

"Well, trust me; your house is on fire. Double back for yourself." I hung up the phone and realized that he was right. It was up to me to find the extinguisher to put out the fire. It was up to me to make the time to live.

Your Assignment

Often when we get busy or overwhelmed the first area we neglect is our own self-care. Contemplate what needs you have been neglecting in your life. Begin devoting time to yourself on a regular basis.

Day 61
Personal Power Cards

❋

"Everything I need to know is revealed to me.
Everything I need comes to me. All is well in my life."
Louise Hay

One of my favorite pick-me-up techniques and self-growth tools are my PERSONAL POWER cards. These are easy and fun to make. Here's the premise: each time you see something that encourages you remember it by recording it on a PERSONAL POWER card. It might be a quote that you find inspiring, lyrics to a song, or an action you would like to take, (*i.e.* try something new each day; take a chance; dream big and love bigger.) Write each of these reminders on an index card. For extra creativity and fun, color, sticker, or print a computer design and paste it to the other side of the card. Visit a scrapbook or stamp store for loads of inspiration and design ideas. Keep these PERSONAL POWER cards with your CYLC Binder. Each day, pick out a few that resonate with you and carry them with you in your CATCH-ALL notebook. Remember to look at them throughout the day as reminders on how you are improving your life.

Your Assignment

Pick up some plain index cards at your office supply store. Look back over the days of your challenge and pick a few reminders you would like to have in your PERSONAL POWER card repertoire. Skim through the quotes within this book for additional positive thoughts. Write the thoughts on blank index cards and decorate. Keep a few blank cards in your CATCH-ALL notebook so you can add quotes and thoughts as you come across them.

✎ I have reprinted my personal power cards in the *Companion Workbook*. Feel free to print, cut, use, and decorate as you desire.

This is a wonderful website containing many positive thoughts that you may want to check out: http://www.yourdailyaffirmation.com/

Day 62
Ten-Minute Retreats

"There must be quite a few things a hot bath won't cure, but I don't know many of them."
Sylvia Plath

As we near the end of the challenge this week, we will be doing some evaluation work on our system and a few last self-care activities. Let's start with "Ten-Minute Retreats."

I believe that every day you should have two "Ten-Minute Retreats" as part of your sanity program! Some days you will be lucky to get one — but try and aim for two. Basically, I define a retreat as: *Ten minutes where you are not engaged in an activity that has any purpose except self-fulfillment.* In other words, you aren't transferring items from your CATCH-ALL notebook, you aren't catching up on laundry, you aren't helping out your partner or children — you are engaged in either relaxation, nature, reading, prayer, meditation, day-dreaming, or a hobby for the purpose of your own self-fulfillment.

Here is why this is so important. Our moods run much like bank accounts. Each area of our life has a separate "register" (spiritual, mental, physical, relationships, self-care, *etc.*). When we do something positive in an area we are making a "deposit" into that register. When we neglect or ignore an area, we are "withdrawing" from the register. Like real bank accounts, if we withdraw too much we overdraft or go bankrupt. When we hit bankrupt (or close to it) we get moody, edgy, short with others, depressed, or fatigued.

When we make appropriate deposits into each of the life areas, our whole life "balances" and our "net statement" becomes positive again.

Your Assignment

Make some deposits into your own "Self Care Account" by aiming for two Ten-Minute Retreats each day.

Day 63
The Power of Visualization

✵

"When one door closes another door opens; but we so often look so long and so regretfully upon the closed door, that we do not see the ones which open for us."
Alexander Graham Bell

Visualization is pretty much what it sounds like — visualizing something in your mind prior to it happening. Many studies have shown that when we visualize something prior to it occurring, we have a greater chance of attaining our desired result. In other words, when we take the time to visualize success we are more apt to meet with success in reality.

Joy Konig, MD, describes visualization as "the active and intentional use of visualization to influence or create a specific outcome or goal. Creative visualization can be used to change our physiological or emotional state, enhance our creativity, and improve our athletic and social skills. It is characterized by the use of a script, whether the script is spoken or read by a trained facilitator, prerecorded, memorized, or created impromptu as part of the imaging process." She has an interesting article that I encourage you to check out at:

http://members.aol.com/thewellnesssite/visualization.htm.

Visualization has been accepted as a very valuable tool in areas from business to medicine. Joy describes many of the physical ailments that visualization has helped with — from cancer to anxiety.

Today I want to give you a couple of examples of how you can use Creative Visualization or Guided Imagery in your own life.

THE NIGHT BEFORE TECHNIQUE: Each night, when you do your master planning, take an additional five minutes to relax. Take deep breaths, inhaling through your nose for the count of five and then exhaling through your mouth to the count of five. Continue to-do this until you feel a sense of calm. Next, imagine the day ahead of you. What will you wear? What will you be doing? What are your goals for the day? Imagine yourself waking in a positive and upbeat mood. See yourself moving through your day with peace and ease, accomplishing all you set out to-do. If you have a speaking engagement or an important conversation, see yourself speaking to the person and imagine what you will say. Play the day in your mind exactly as you hope it to play-out in reality. Continue this every evening for 21 days and pay attention to what happens. You may want to keep a journal of how your visualized days go — I think you will be surprised with how closely they mirror your imagery! Whenever I do my visualization work, I also always ask for God's guidance. I ask that He guide my words and actions each day. I also begin each day with a simple prayer that reflects that. (In fact one of my favorite POWER CARDS simply says, "God, guide my every thought, deed, and action." I repeat this to myself throughout the day, whenever I feel stress, sadness, frustration, or anger creeping into my heart.

THE TURN-IT OVER TECHNIQUE: This technique can be helpful when something is weighing heavily on your shoulders. It allows us to "let it go." Visualize the problem as clearly as possible. What does the scene feel like? Smell like? Look like? Once you have completely visualized your problem, see a large balloon coming down and surrounding the scene. Then imagine the problem being lifted and floating away from you. Turn it over to God or your Higher Power for help. This is simply a visual exercise to enforce the powerful saying, "LET GO AND LET GOD."

Your Assignment

Try one of these visualization exercises today. Remember to add these techniques to your tool kit for facing life's challenges.

Day 64
Self-Sabotage

✵

"You've got to jump off cliffs all the time
and build your wings on the way down."
Ray Bradbury

As we near the end of the program I thought it important to address the dreaded act of "SELF-SABOTAGE." Self-sabotage often lurks in the shadows, dashing our hopes or impeding our plans. Other times, it is like a semi-truck, careening right into us. Perhaps you've already felt a bit of self-sabotage as you worked through the program — or perhaps, there will be some around the corner. Here are some common examples of how self-sabotage surfaces in a woman's life:

OFF TO A ROARING START — AT FIRST: You begin something new — whether it be an exercise program, the Change Your Life Challenge, or a new eating regimen. The first two days go perfectly smooth and then you hit a block of some sort — a child is sick, or a nice dinner with your favorite dessert is served. You momentarily lapse into old patterns and then the voice of self-sabotage says: "See... I told you. You can't do it." Instead of restarting the next day, you just push your goal aside into a junk drawer.

IF THIS HAPPENS TO YOU: Realize that it is self-sabotage at work. You deserve more. You deserve the changes you want — and you *can* achieve them. It's okay to slip, to fall, to bruise your knees, but then re-start the next day. Restart without guilt or self-criticism.

WE CHANGE ... FOR A WHILE: We implement a new change in our life — and it works for us. But after a while we decide it is just too much work to change our ways and revert to old patterns.

IF THIS HAPPENS TO YOU: Again, self-sabotage is at play. Remember that when we keep doing what we have always done, we keep getting what we always got. You wanted change. That's why you are taking this challenge. Kick self-sabotage to the curb and continue with your program. Or if you need to take a day or two off, do so and then continue onward.

WE START FORWARD ... ONLY TO BE PULLED BACKWARD BY OUR PAST: We might start down a new path and then find ourselves feeling "blue" or "blah" shortly into our journey. Often, the root of this "blah" feeling is our inability to forgive ourselves. We might make a mistake on the journey and be uncompromising in our demand for perfection. This conflict can lead to abandoning our new endeavor. Or perhaps something from the past has left us feeling we are undeserving. Maybe we made a mistake, hurt someone, or hurt ourselves. Instead of working through this past event, we suppress it and it resurfaces as self-sabotage.

IF THIS HAPPENS TO YOU: Your in luck, this book contains an entire intermission devoted to forgiveness—of both self and others. Take some time to work through the intermission to lay this past event to rest once and for all.

Your Daily Assignment

Has self-sabotage affected your progress? If so, how? Now that you can give it a name, how will you kick self-sabotage to the curb? One of the easiest ways is through support and encouragement of others. Visit the CYLC website. Kind words of others will remind you of all you can achieve! An encouraging statement from one CYLC member: "Changing require courage ... staying the same does not."

Day 65

Become a Lifelong Learner

"Twenty years from now you will be more disap-
pointed by the things that you didn't do than by the ones you did do. So throw off the bowlines. Sail away from the safe harbor. Catch the trade winds in your sails. Explore. Dream. Discover."

Mark Twain

I have always had a love of learning. I loved learning when I was young and the passion to acquire knowledge has stayed with me throughout the years. I love the process of taking the unfamiliar and watching it transform to the familiar. In fact, just two weeks ago I started learning electric guitar. (I play a great rendition of OLD MCDONALD.) In any case, when we learn, we exercise our mind and our childlike sense of discovery. Some studies point to learning as a valid tool for repressing Alzheimer's disease. Learning is "exercise for the brain."

There are so many ways to learn. We can learn online, from books, from computer tutorials, at community classes, YMCAs, workshops — you name it, learning is everywhere!

Learning something you enjoy is also a great stress reliever. I can't tell you how much I enjoy pounding out some off-key chords after a long and stressful day. People find stress-release in all sorts of learning experiences — the arts, photography, sports. With so many ways to learn, there isn't the issue of time that once used to dictate our learning. If you can't get to a class, then bring the class to you through the Internet, an instructional DVD, or computer software. I just completed my first songwriting class from the Berkley School of Music through their Internet offerings. Barnesandnoble.com also has a B&N University that has many wonderful free classes taught by a variety of experts through the Internet. Visit www.bn.com to learn more. My friend Carrie Myers Smith offers several free classes on health and goal setting and her website, www.womeninwellness.com.

Your Assignment

Make a list of topics or interests that you would like to learn more about. Then investigate possible options for learning. Is there an online course? Could you order a book or software? (Try a search at www.amazon.com on your given topic or at www.google.com.) Are there classes in your community? Choose one topic to pursue and then layout a plan for learning.

✎ See the *Companion Workbook* for a detailed list of online learning opportunities.

Day 66
Take A Chance

"Far better it is to dare mighty things, to win glorious triumphs, even though checkered by failure, than to take rank with those poor souls who neither enjoy much nor suffer much, because they live in the gray twilight that knows neither victory nor defeat."
Theodore Roosevelt

Ever feel like each day is the same-old, same-old? Well the unfortunate truth is that if you don't take the steps to spice up your life, it probably won't get any spicier! Since we are now focusing on *you*, here is a strategy for adding fun and flair to your life.

Write down five things you would like to-do, which you normally would NOT do. This list can include anything. Perhaps you want to express your true feelings to someone. Perhaps you want to finish a painting that has been in the attic for ten years. Perhaps you want to try a new recipe but never find the time. Don't do this exercise in a rush. Take the time to *really* consider five things that you would *really* like to-do, but normally wouldn't.

Your Assignment

Pick one item of the five and do it! Whenever you feel those familiar blues coming back, take a step away from them by doing something out of the ordinary. Remember, we only keep getting the same results when we keep doing what we've always done. Change what you are doing and your results will change too! Add to this list continually and refer back to it whenever you need some fun and flair in your life.

✎ See the *Companion Workbook* for a "Take a Chance" inventory worksheet.

Intermission: Girls' Night Out

When I began the task of putting this challenge together, I spent a great deal of time examining those months in my life when I felt the most fulfilled. I looked for the common denominators among those periods. I noticed that during my most fulfilled times, I regularly had a "Girls' Night Out."

In my life, if I don't have "a standing" appointment, something is likely to get pushed to the side. Although I often intend to get together with a group of girlfriends, intentions too often dissolve into "yesterdays." Establishing a regular night "out with the girls" guarantees a good laugh, adult conversation, and social time with a trusted circle.

When I lived in Portland, we had a "Bunco" group. Bunco is a very simple dice game that anyone can learn in less than five minutes. It doesn't require a ton of focus, so it is easy to talk and share while playing. We had about twenty women in this group and throughout the night we rotated tables, allowing for plenty of interaction.

At another time, I joined a bowling league. Although I am one of the world's worst bowlers, it was fun to get out with a group of six women and enjoy a few hours of laughter, sharing, and gaming fun.

Each year, I regularly take a weekend away with my best friend. We plan a relaxing weekend free of schedules, deadlines, and demands.

Before I had my daughter, I regularly met a woman (or group of women) for coffee each morning at our local café.

Whether it be once a week, or monthly, spending time with other women helps us to live our own lives more effectively. We can learn from one another, share with one another, and support one another. Consider starting your own "Girls' Night Out" regimen.

Part Eleven

Something More

Days 67 and 68

- ☐ Complete your gratitude journal each evening.
- ☐ Begin each day with a heartfelt "good morning."
- ☐ Carry your CATCH-ALL notebook with you everywhere.
- ☐ Transfer your to-do list each night.
- ☐ Complete your Nightly Reflection each evening.
- ☐ Each day, use the three-step action list.
- ☐ Consult your MASTER TASK LISTS for any other tasks that need to be completed.
- ☐ Do a daily laundry load if volume warrants.
- ☐ Host a daily "Happy Half-Hour."
- ☐ Practice the Five-Minute Relationship Miracle daily.
- ☐ Review your "value-card" daily.
- ☐ Give your children a self-esteem booster each day.
- ☐ Follow your morning routine.
- ☐ Use your "value number" to evaluate all of your spending.
- ☐ Drink at least eight, (8 oz.) glasses of water today.
- ☐ Incorporate your "starting level" of daily exercise.
- ☐ Have a healthy breakfast.
- ☐ Add some fruit and veggies to your meals today.
- ☐ Eat all of your meals and snacks at the table.
- ☐ Choose a "Personal Power Card" to carry with you daily.
- ☐ Take at least one ten-minute retreat today.
- ☐ Visualize tomorrow before going to sleep tonight.

Day 69

- ☐ Complete your gratitude journal each evening.
- ☐ Begin each day with a heartfelt "good morning."
- ☐ Carry your CATCH-ALL notebook with you everywhere.
- ☐ Transfer your to-do list each night.
- ☐ Complete your Nightly Reflection each evening.
- ☐ Each day, use the three-step action list.
- ☐ Consult your MASTER TASK LISTS for any other tasks that need to be completed.
- ☐ Do a daily laundry load if volume warrants.
- ☐ Host a daily "Happy Half-Hour."

- ☐ Practice the Five-Minute Relationship Miracle daily.
- ☐ Review your "value-card" daily.
- ☐ Give your children a self-esteem booster each day.
- ☐ Follow your morning routine.
- ☐ Use your "value number" to evaluate all of your spending.
- ☐ Drink at least eight, (8 oz.) glasses of water today.
- ☐ Incorporate your "starting level" of daily exercise.
- ☐ Have a healthy breakfast.
- ☐ Add some fruit and veggies to your meals today.
- ☐ Eat all of your meals and snacks at the table.
- ☐ Choose a "Personal Power Card" to carry with you daily.
- ☐ Take at least one ten-minute retreat today.
- ☐ Visualize tomorrow before going to sleep tonight.
- ☐ Take a short break each day to find a moment or two of peace.

Day 67
Philanthropy

✵

"I always had a dream that when I am asked to give an accounting of my life to a higher court, it will be like this: So, empty your pockets. What have you got left of your life? Any dreams that were unfilled? Any unused talent we gave you when you were born that you have left? Any unsaid compliments or bits of love that you haven't spread around?
And I will answer, " I have nothing to return.
I spent everything you gave me.
I'm as naked as the day I was born."
Erma Bombeck

As I built this challenge, I spent a great deal of time analyzing at which points in my life I felt the most complete. Not that I am incomplete, but you know the times I speak of, those times where you are "in the zone," or "more balanced" than at other times. As I recalled these harmonic times, I sought out the common denominators that they shared. During all my periods of contentment, I was heavily involved in volunteer efforts of some kind.

I have helped out with different student organizations such as Girl Scouts and 4-H. I have created and coordinate plays for youth groups. My Mom tells a story where at age ten I put on a bake sale and sold $300 worth of cookies so I could send the money to help repair the Statue of Liberty. (My arm grew tired after mixing one batch of cookie dough, so my mom helped with the rest. Perhaps that is why her memory of this event is so vivid.)

A few Christmas' back, I noticed that I experienced the "holiday blues" in a more pronounced way than previous years. The holidays had come upon me so quickly and then in a flash they were gone. When I looked for the source of my sadness, I realized that I had been so busy with work endeavors that year, I had not engaged in leading any gift or food-roundup programs or played "Secret Santa" to a needy family. I hadn't partaken in Christmas caroling or other activities that fill us with the warmth that only giving can give.

The greatest gift we can ever give is our self. It is a gift no one else can duplicate. Whether it's weekly, monthly, quarterly, or yearly, giving of ourselves connects us to the world around us.

Your Assignment

Choose a cause where you would like to contribute your energies. Set a goal for your contribution over the course of the next year, whether it be weekly, monthly, quarterly, or yearly.

Day 68

Connect to Something Bigger than Yourself

✵

"If you change the way you look at things,
the things you look at change."
Author Unknown

Minutes quickly turn to hours, hours quickly turn to days, days quickly turn to months. If we don't create moments in our lives to pause and reflect, the days will disappear as we cruise on autopilot — a passenger to our own life.

Many people experience this sensation at the end of each year. "Where did the year go?" "Can you believe it's 200__ already?"

To actively participate and enjoy our own lives we must make time to pause and center ourselves. These moments of reflection must be as engrained in our schedules just as getting dressed and brushing our teeth.

When my brother was living, he started each day by walking out onto the deck of our childhood home and looking out over the lake. I never asked Caleb what exactly he was looking at, or looking for, if anything.

This past year, I began walking outside every morning prior to everyone in my house waking. Much like my brother, I would just reflect on nature for a minute or two before starting my day. As I repeated this activity day after day, I have become convinced that he was connecting to "something bigger," absorbing a bit of the peace and magic that can only be found in nature — into his own life and soul.

Your Assignment

For the next thirty days, begin each day with a two-minute "pause" outside. Have nothing on your agenda accept absorbing some of the magic and peace that can be found in nature.

Day 69
What Do You See?

"Two men look out the same prison bars; one sees mud and the other stars."
Frederick Langbridge

Something interesting happened to me today. It is New Years Day, so perhaps I am a bit more reflective than usual as I make resolutions and busily reflect on the year gone by.

I was contemplating one of my favorite questions, "What makes us truly happy?" Not fleeting happiness, but that type of happiness that runs so deep it tingles the soul. I was asking this question while emptying the dishwasher and putting in a new load of dishes.

As odd as it sounds, I was placing a small periwinkle serving plate onto the lower shelf and couldn't recall a time I had been happier. Then I realized why I was finding such complete satisfaction in such a simple activity.

I didn't see "loading the dishwasher" as yet another chore that needed to be completed. Instead, as I emptied and loaded, I stayed present in the moment, really absorbing and enjoying each step I took. In doing so, the periwinkle plate had taken on a meeting much more profound than a "dirty dish." The plate represented how fortunate my family is to have such wonderful and bountiful meals. It represented the family dinner, and how fortunate we are to have our health and each other. (A blessing that is magnified as we watch the horrendous tsunami disaster in Asia.)

How quickly an often-loathed task had become a reason to celebrate all the joys in life.

Your Assignment

Try looking beyond the "obvious" today. Think outside the box while you complete daily routines and activities. Find reasons to experience joy and gratitude in unexpected places.

Day 70
Analyzing Your System and the Certificate of Sanity

"It's not so important who starts the game
but who finishes it."
John Wooden

As you prepare to move on after the CYLC I want to take a moment and evaluate the past 70 days in detail. First, we are going to explore the Monthly Task Worksheet and Yearly Task Worksheet you have been working from.

If you have followed the program directions, you have been using this system for a solid six weeks. These lists are your "home base," your reference for life and home maintenance. It's important that this sheet works for you, so let's examine any adjustments that you may choose to make.

Rewrite your tasks onto the Evaluating Your Task List worksheet in the appendix. Follow the instructions for assessing each task. Use your answers to make any needed revisions.

✎ See the *Companion Workbook* for additional copies of these Task List Worksheets and the question and answer blanks.

Certificate of Sanity

Now let's analyze the progress you have made as a whole. In the first column below, list your rating from when you completed your Before Snapshot during our first day together. In the second column, write the results from the worksheet you just completed. In the third column, net out how you changed in each area, whether positively or negatively. For example, if your HOME MANAGEMENT was a two when you started and now you rate yourself a five, give yourself a +3 in column three.

Area	Rating at beginning of program	Rating at Day 70	Amount of Change (+5, -2, etc.)
Finances			
Friendships			
Relationship with Kids			
Home Management			
Exercise			
Nutrition			
Time Management			
Time for Self			
Spiritual Life			
Relationship with Partner			
Work Life			

After you have completed the exercise on the previous page, answer the following questions.

1. In what two areas have you seen the most change? What has changed and how does that make you feel?

Area of Change

____

Changes and Feelings

____

____

____

Area of Change

____

Changes and Feelings

____

____

____

2. Did this exercise reveal anything that surprised you?

____

____

____

3. How do you feel about your progress?

4. In what areas did you not fair so well and why do you think that is?

5. What days could you go back and do again to help you in the areas mentioned in Question 4?

6. When (specifically) will you go back and do the days needed for Questions 4 and 5?

____

____

____

7. How do you plan on maintaining the progress you have made now that the program is over?

____

____

____

To receive your certificate of sanity, please provide a photocopy of the analysis done in Day 70. Mail this information to: The Change Your Life Challenge, c/o Champion Press, Ltd., 4308 Blueberry Road, Fredonia WI 53021. Make sure to include:

Name
Address
City, State, Zip
E-mail:

Note: Your First Name, City, and State will be listed on the web site as a 70-DAY CHALLENGE GRADUATE. You'll also receive a special tips booklet with your certificate.

Final Thoughts ...

Over the weekend, I had an interesting conversation with a dear friend. We were discussing why we sometimes "enter funks" when we are perfectly capable of reaching our goals and making changes. In some ways, life is actually quite easy, yet we make it more difficult. If we break down our goals and take simple steps, we can accomplish just about anything.

When I reflected on this conversation later that evening, I had an interesting insight. Perhaps we don't take steps toward our "happy ever after," because what happens if once we get there – our "happy ever after" isn't so happy? It is another way of saying, "the demons that you know are better than the demons that you don't." Both of these statements reflect the importance of focusing on now, each day, each hour, each second.

However, you are not in the "masses." You have completed an aggressive and life-changing 70-Day program. Change doesn't happen tomorrow, it happens when you take hold of today.

Appendix

Worksheets:

Before Snapshot *(use with Day One assignment)*

Relationship with partner	Spiritual life	Time for self	Time management	Nutrition	Exercise	Home management	Relationship with kids	Friendships	Finances
1	1	1	1	1	1	1	1	1	1
2	2	2	2	2	2	2	2	2	2
3	3	3	3	3	3	3	3	3	3
4	4	4	4	4	4	4	4	4	4
5	5	5	5	5	5	5	5	5	5
6	6	6	6	6	6	6	6	6	6
7	7	7	7	7	7	7	7	7	7
8	8	8	8	8	8	8	8	8	8
9	9	9	9	9	9	9	9	9	9
10	10	10	10	10	10	10	10	10	10

Monthly Task List and Yearly Task List

Due to size constraints, this worksheet appears on two pages in this book. A one-page version can be downloaded off the web site at www.changeyourlifechallenge.com or found in the *Companion Workbook.*

MONTHLY TASK LIST

Task	Task "Master"	1	2	3	4	5	6	7	8	9	10	11	12	13	14	15

MONTHLY TASK LIST (PART TWO)

Task	Task "Master"	16	17	18	19	20	21	22	23	24	25	26	27	28	29	30	31

YEARLY TASK LIST

Task	Task “Master”	JAN	FEB	MAR	APR	MAY	JUNE	JUL	AUG	SEP	OCT	NOV	DEC

ORGANIZING OUR RELATIONSHIPS

Name	How much time do I spend with him/her each week?	Personality Rating	Change to Be Made	Card Communication

PRIORITIZING OUR RELATIONSHIPS

A. People I need to spend more time with	B. People who can remain at status quo	C. People I need to spend less time with

Visit

www.championpress.com

to view other life and time-management titles, and other books by Brook Noel, or to download the *Change Your Life Challenge Companion Workbook*